English Olympiad

Highly useful for all school students participating
in Various Olympiads & Competitions

Series Editor Keshav Mohan

Authors Amit Tanwar & Summi Grover

Class
3

ARIHANT PRAKASHAN, MEERUT

ARIHANT PRAKASHAN, MEERUT

卐 Administrative & Production Offices

Regd. Office 'Ramchhaya' 4577/15, Agarwal Road, Darya Ganj New Delhi -110002
Tele: 011- 47630600, 43518550; Fax: 011- 23280316

Head Office Kalindi, TP Nagar, Meerut (UP) - 250002
Tele: 0121-2401479, 2512970, 4004199; Fax: 0121-2401648

All disputes subject to Meerut (UP) jurisdiction only.

卐 Sales & Support Offices

Agra, Ahmedabad, Bengaluru, Bhubaneswar, Bareilly, Chennai, Delhi, Guwahati, Haldwani, Hyderabad, Jaipur, Jhansi, Kolkata, Kota, Lucknow, Meerut, Nagpur & Pune

卐 ISBN 978-93-5094-429-5

卐 Price ₹50.00

Typeset by Arihant DTP Unit at Meerut
Printed & Bound by Arihant Publications (I) Ltd. (Press Unit)

Production Team

Publishing Manager	Mahendra Singh Rawat	*DTP Operator*	Akash Deep
Project Head	Shivani Solan	*Cover Designer*	Syed Darin Zaidi
Proof Readers	Mandeep & Anu Priya	*Inner Designer*	Deepak Kumar
Page Layouting	Subodh Kumar		

For further information about the products from Arihant
log on to www.arihantbooks.com or email to info@arihantbooks.com

Preface

English Olympiad Series for Class 1st -10th is a series of books which will challenge the young inquisitive minds by the non-routine and exciting Questions on the use of English.

The main purpose of this series is to make the students ready for competitive exams, as English Language is an integral section of almost all competitive examinations. All the questions given in this series are objective in nature so they will provide students a feel of competitive examinations as school/board exams are of qualifying nature but not competitive, which mainly have objective questions.

- **Need of Olympiad Series**
  This series helps students who are willing to sharpen their proficiency in the field of English language. Unlike typical assessment books, which emphasise on drilling practice, the focus of this series is on practising problem solving techniques. It will help the students use the concepts they have learnt to discover that they can actually solve questions.

- **Development of Communication Skills**
  Application based questions given in this series will help students to attain a deeper understanding of different concepts of English Language through which students will be able to imbibe more effective communication skills in themselves.

- **Complement Your School Studies**
  This series complements the additional preparation needs of students for regular school/board exams. By learning English effectively, students will not only be able to perform well in English language exam but also they will perform better in Science/Social Science/Mathematics where medium to write the answer is English. Along with, it will also address all the requirements of the students who are approaching National/State level Olympiads.

I shall welcome criticism from the students, teachers, educators and parents. I shall also like to hear from all of you about errors and shortcomings which may have remained in this edition and the suggestions for their improvement in the next edition.

Editor

Contents

Sentence and Its Types

Directions (Q. Nos. 1-7) *Identify the predicate in the given sentences.*

1. My father drives his car.
(a) drives (b) my father
(c) drives his car (d) car

2. A good child never tells a lie.
(a) a good child (b) never tells a lie
(c) never tells (d) a lie

3. The Himalayas is the highest mountain range.
(a) the Himalayas
(b) is the
(c) highest mountain range
(d) is the highest mountain range

4. Birds enjoy freedom.
(a) birds enjoy (b) freedom
(c) enjoy freedom (d) None of these

5. The ocean has many fishes.
(a) has many fishes (b) ocean
(c) has (d) many fishes

6. Holi is the festival of colours.
(a) holi is the
(b) holi is the festival
(c) is the festival of colours
(d) of colours

7. Jack and Mary live in the same building.
(a) Jack and Mary
(b) Mary live in the
(c) live in the same
(d) live in the same building

8. Match the following subjects with their predicates.

	Subject		Predicate
A.	Laughter	1.	is my favourite teacher.
B.	Ms Teena	2.	created all of us.
C.	Children	3.	is the best medicine.
D.	God	4.	like to play.

Codes

	A	B	C	D
(a)	1	2	3	4
(b)	3	1	4	2
(c)	4	2	1	3
(d)	2	1	4	3

Directions (Q. Nos. 9-18) *Identify the kind of sentence by choosing from the given options.*

9. Are you planning to visit a few places around Chennai?
(a) Assertive (b) Interrogative
(c) Exclamatory (d) Imperative

10. I want to go to Mahabalipuram.
(a) Interrogative (b) Exclamatory
(c) Assertive (d) Imperative

11. Oh no! I dropped my chocolate.
(a) Imperative (b) Exclamatory
(c) Assertive (d) Interrogative

12. Peter, do not make a noise, said the teacher.
(a) Imperative (b) Assertive
(c) Interrogative (d) Exclamatory

13. The peon did not ring the bell.
(a) Imperative
(b) Negative
(c) Exclamatory
(d) Assertive

14. What a fantastic performance by the Rock band!
(a) Assertive (b) Exclamatory
(c) Interrogative (d) Imperative

15. Would you like to have tea or coffee?
(a) Assertive (b) Exclamatory
(c) Imperative (d) Interrogative

16. John did not break another glass today.
(a) Negative
(b) Interrogative
(c) Imperative
(d) Exclamatory

17. John said that he will not do his homework.
(a) Interrogative
(b) Imperative
(c) Assertive
(d) Exclamatory

18. What a bliss! to spend time in natural surroundings!
(a) Assertive
(b) Exclamatory
(c) Interrogative
(d) Imperative

Directions (Q. Nos. 19-27) *Do as directed and choose the correct option for the given sentences.*

19. Identify the interrogative sentence.
(a) Wow! my mother is a doctor!
(b) My mother is a doctor.
(c) Is my mother a doctor?
(d) None of the above

20. Identify the negative sentence.
(a) I will go to school today.
(b) I will not go to school today.
(c) Will I go to school today?
(d) I will go to school today!

21. Identify an exclamatory sentence.
(a) I am so excited.
(b) Am I so excited?
(c) I am so excited!
(d) I am not so excited.

22. Identify an imperative sentence.
(a) Maintain silence.
(b) Can you maintain silence?
(c) Do not maintain silence.
(d) Maintain silence!

23. Identify an assertive/declarative sentence.
(a) Tom and Harry will watch a movie.
(b) Tom and Harry will not watch a movie.
(c) Will Tom and Harry watch a movie?
(d) None of the above

24. Identify the interrogative sentence.
(a) You have deposited the fees!
(b) Have you deposited the fees?
(c) You have not deposited the fees.
(d) You have deposited the fees.

25. Identify an imperative sentence.
(a) We should obey traffic rules!
(b) We should not obey traffic rules.
(c) We should obey traffic rules.
(d) Should we obey traffic rules?

26. Identify an exclamatory sentence.

(a) Hema did not win the lottery.
(b) Hema won the lottery.
(c) Did Hema win the lottery?
(d) Hema just won the lottery!

27. Identify negative sentence.

(a) It will not rain tomorrow.
(b) Will it rain tomorrow?
(c) It will rain tomorrow!
(d) It will rain tomorrow.

28. Match the following sentences with their types.

	List I		List II
A.	Why didn't you come to school today?	1.	Assertive
B.	Please pass the salt.	2.	Interrogative
C.	I love you so much!	3.	Imperative
D.	I am ten years old and love my school very much.	4.	Exclamatory

Codes

	A	B	C	D		A	B	C	D
(a)	3	2	1	4	(b)	2	3	4	1
(c)	1	4	2	3	(d)	2	1	4	3

Directions (Q. Nos. 29-35) *Given below is a paragraph. Read it carefully and complete the paragraph by filling the blanks with suitable subject and predicate.*

Jack was. ...**(29)**.... It was the first time he was boarding a ship. This was ...**(30)**.... It was full of books! He saw many shelves of books in the main area. ...**(31)**... had books on culture, music, art, history, fiction etc. Fiction books ...**(32)**... . So, he decided ...**(33)**... . He decided that he would also buy a book for his cousin Mary. Mary loves ...**(34)**.... Both of them will read lots of stories ...**(35)**.... Thinking of this idea, Jack left happily.

29. (a) nice place (b) very excited
(c) is exciting (d) exciting

30. (a) an extraordinary ship
(b) ship
(c) water boat
(d) small ship

31. (a) He (b) Ship
(c) The shelves (d) Stories

32. (a) many books (b) collected them
(c) nervous (d) fascinated him

33. (a) to buy three books (b) no book
(c) any book (d) book

34. (a) to eating
(b) in stories
(c) to read children's stories
(d) on books

35. (a) on story books
(b) fiction books
(c) vacations
(d) in the vacations

Answers

1. (c)	**2.** (b)	**3.** (d)	**4.** (c)	**5.** (a)	**6.** (c)	**7.** (d)	**8.** (b)	**9.** (b)	**10.** (c)
11. (b)	**12.** (a)	**13.** (b)	**14.** (b)	**15.** (d)	**16.** (a)	**17.** (c)	**18.** (b)	**19.** (c)	**20.** (b)
21. (c)	**22.** (a)	**23.** (a)	**24.** (b)	**25.** (c)	**26.** (d)	**27.** (a)	**28.** (b)	**29.** (b)	**30.** (a)
31. (c)	**32.** (d)	**33.** (a)	**34.** (c)	**35.** (d)					

Noun

Directions (Q. Nos. 1-5) *Identify the common noun in the following sentences.*

1. All boys like to play football.
(a) like (b) boys
(c) play (d) football

2. I visited a big city.
(a) visited (b) a
(c) big (d) city

3. My family will go to the restaurant.
(a) my (b) will
(c) restaurant (d) go

4. The dogs bark at night.
(a) dogs (b) bark
(c) at (d) night

5. Keep the books on my table.
(a) keep (b) books
(c) on (d) my

Directions (Q. Nos. 6-8) *Fill in the blanks with suitable collective noun choosing from the given options.*

6. Yesterday, I lost my .... of keys.
(a) bouquet (b) bundle
(c) bunch (d) packet

7. We saw a .... of sheep on our way to home.
(a) fleet
(b) flock
(c) colony
(d) flight

8. A .... of cattle was grazing.
(a) team
(b) crowd
(c) herd
(d) packet

Directions (Q. Nos. 9-13) *Fill in the blanks with appropriate collective noun.*

9. He gave me a .... of grapes.

(a) box
(b) bunch
(c) bouquet
(d) herd

10. The principal formed a .... for Annual day function.

(a) meeting (b) group
(c) committee (d) crowd

11. Indian .... is proud of its soldier.

(a) fleet (b) army
(c) committee (d) crowd

12. Students presented a .... of flowers to their class teacher.

(a) bunch (b) fleet
(c) bouquet (d) herd

13. On Sundays there is a big .... in malls.

(a) mob (b) crowd
(c) fleet (d) bunch

Directions (Q. Nos. 14-18) *Choose the correct abstract noun for the given word.*

14. Kind
(a) Kindery (b) Kindness
(c) Kindly (d) Kindment

15. Wise
(a) Wisely (b) Wiseness
(c) Wisdom (d) Wisehood

16. Loyal
(a) Loyalty (b) Loyally
(c) Loyable (d) Loyalness

17. Sick
(a) Sicker (b) Sickment
(c) Sickness (d) Sickhood

18. Friend
(a) Friendless
(b) Friendship
(c) Friendy
(d) Friendhood

Directions (Q. Nos. 19-23) *Choose the option which is the correct example of the given word.*

19. Countable noun
(a) Milk (b) Oil
(c) Sugar (d) Book

20. Uncountable noun
(a) Pen (b) Table
(c) Milk (d) Sister

21. Countable noun
(a) Honesty (b) Boy
(c) Gold (d) Oil

22. Uncountable noun
(a) Poverty (b) Doctor
(c) Uncle (d) Bowl

23. Countable noun
(a) Flour (b) Stars
(c) Water (d) Teacher

Directions (Q. Nos. 24-27) *Read the words given below and identify their plural form from the given options.*

24. Buffalo

(a) Buffalos (b) Buffales
(c) Buffaloes (d) Buffalse

25. Shelf

(a) Shelfs (b) Shelves
(c) Shelfes (d) Shelfse

26. Cactus

(a) Cactuss (b) Cactuses
(c) Cactus (d) Cacti

27. Knife

(a) Knifes (b) Knifse
(c) Knives (d) Knifese

Directions (Q. Nos. 28-31) *Read the words given below and identify their singular form from the given options.*

28. Mice

(a) Mousse (b) Mouses
(c) Mouse (d) Mices

29. Heroes

(a) Heros (b) Hero
(c) Herose (d) Heroese

30. Stories

(a) Stori (b) Storis
(c) Story (d) Storise

31. Teeth

(a) Teeths
(b) Tooth
(c) Tooths
(d) Toothse

Directions (Q. Nos. 32-36) *Choose the correct opposite gender of the given word.*

32. Emperor

(a) Emperoress (b) Empriss
(c) Empress (d) She smperor

33. Bull

(a) Vixen (b) Cow
(c) Bullock (d) Buffalo

34. Nephew

(a) Niece (b) Brother
(c) Sister (d) Cousin

35. Tigress

(a) Lion (b) Tiger
(c) Cub (d) Lioness

36. Peacock

(a) Peachick (b) Peadon
(c) Pearess (d) Peahen

Directions (Q. Nos. 37-43) *Read the passage given below which has some blanks. Fill in the blanks to complete the passage. Choose from the given options.*

Mother Earth has given us many gifts. One of them is trees. ...**(37)**... are very important to us. Many of our tribes live inside ...**(38)**... which have trees. Trees provide us wood to make ...**(39)**... . Wild animals depend on trees for ...**(40)**... and shelter. Trees help us to prevent soil erosion and floods.

They give out ...**(41)**... and make the Earth clean and cool. Many products such as paper, gum, rubber etc are obtained from trees.

Trees reduce ...**(42)**... and increase rain. Birds make their ...**(43)**... on trees. So friends save trees by not cutting them and make them happy.

37. (a) Earth (b) Forest (c) Plants (d) Trees

38. (a) trees (b) forests (c) caves (d) houses

39. (a) house (b) park (c) furniture (d) huts

40. (a) fruits (b) flowers (c) food (d) water

41. (a) carbon oxide (b) oxygen (c) nitrogen (d) nice smell

42. (a) carbon (b) noise (c) dust (d) pollution

43. (a) house (b) food (c) nests (d) resting place

Directions (Q. Nos. 44-45) *Read the passage given below and answer the questions.*

Rahim is from Jammu and Kashmir. He reached Delhi on Friday. He has made a list of all the monuments and temples where he wants to visit in the city. He is very excited to see the Lotus Temple. He also plans to visit his aunt and enjoy with his cousins.

44. How many proper nouns are there in the above passage?
(a) 4 (b) 5 (c) 8 (d) 7

45. How many common nouns are there in the above passage?
(a) 3 (b) 2 (c) 5 (d) 7

Answers

1. (b)	2. (d)	3. (c)	4. (a)	5. (b)	6. (c)	7. (b)	8. (c)	9. (b)	10. (c)
11. (b)	12. (c)	13. (b)	14. (b)	15. (c)	16. (a)	17. (c)	18. (b)	19. (d)	20. (c)
21. (b)	22. (a)	23. (d)	24. (c)	25. (b)	26. (d)	27. (c)	28. (c)	29. (b)	30. (c)
31. (b)	32. (c)	33. (b)	34. (a)	35. (b)	36. (d)	37. (d)	38. (b)	39. (c)	40. (c)
41. (b)	42. (d)	43. (c)	44. (b)	45. (c)					

Pronoun

Directions (Q. Nos. 1-6) *Choose the correct personal pronoun to complete the sentences given below.*

1. My brother loves to eat burgers. This burger is for ....

(a) her (b) them
(c) him (d) he

2. These are my pets. I love ....

(a) this (b) them
(c) we (d) her

3. I cannot lift this box. Could you help ...., please?

(a) me (b) him
(c) her (d) we

4. My sister and I love sweets. These candies are for.......... .

(a) her (b) them
(c) us (d) me

5. Sita is going to the market. .... has to buy vegetables.

(a) He
(b) She
(c) We
(d) They

6. Sam and Tina are classmates. .... are always seen together.

(a) They (b) We
(c) That (d) She

Directions (Q. Nos. 7-11) *Choose the correct interrogative pronoun to complete the given sentences.*

7. .... is the matter?

(a) What (b) Whose
(c) Which (d) Whom

8. Hello, may I know .... is speaking?

(a) which (b) what
(c) who (d) whom

9. .... are you going to invite?

(a) What (b) Whom
(c) Who (d) Which

10. .... is my favourite doll?

(a) Whose (b) Where
(c) Whom (d) Which

11. .... of these books is yours?

(a) Who (b) Why
(c) What (d) Which

Directions (Q. Nos. 12-16) *What can be the correct pronoun for the underlined words.*

12. <u>An ice-cream truck</u> drove down the street.

(a) They (b) Her
(c) It (d) Him

13. Do you want to go to the party with <u>Hanna and Julie</u>?

(a) her (b) we
(c) they (d) them

14. <u>Lizandra</u> is writing a report on Thomas Elva Edison.

(a) Them (b) It
(c) Her (d) She

15. <u>Peter</u> can speak English very well.

(a) Her (b) He
(c) We (d) You

16. <u>Jack and Rosy</u> will visit the museum tomorrow.

(a) He (b) That
(c) They (d) She

Directions (Q. Nos. 17-23) *Fill in the blanks with appropriate reflexive pronouns.*

17. Let me introduce .... My name is Alan.

(a) yourself (b) himself
(c) myself (d) herself

18. How could you do something like that. You must be ashamed of.......... .

(a) himself (b) yourself
(c) myself (d) ourselves

19. The newly appointed MLA tried to help people ....

(a) herself
(b) himself
(c) yourself
(d) myself

20. She weighs .... every morning as she is very conscious of her weight.

(a) himself (b) herself
(c) ourselves (d) myself

21. The children said that they will do it ....

(a) themselves (b) itself
(c) herself (d) yourself

22. The horse slipped and hurt ....

(a) myself (b) herself
(c) itself (d) himself

23. Do not play with fire, you will hurt ....

(a) himself (b) yourself
(c) ourselves (d) myself

24. Match the nouns of List I with their pronouns from List II.

List I	List II
A. <u>Kevin and Martin</u> are going to Nainital.	1. We
B. <u>Joseph</u> studies in a nearby school.	2. It
C. <u>The box</u> is kept in a corner.	3. They
D. <u>Pat and I</u> study together.	4. He

Codes

	A	B	C	D		A	B	C	D
(a)	3	2	1	4	(b)	4	3	1	2
(c)	3	4	2	1	(d)	1	3	2	4

25. Match the interrogative pronouns of List II with the sentences of List I.

List I	List II
A. .... colour is the frog?	1. Who
B. .... does Alice live?	2. Whose
C. .... are these children?	3. What
D. .... is that-little house?	4. Where

Codes

	A	B	C	D		A	B	C	D
(a)	2	4	1	3	(b)	3	4	1	2
(c)	2	3	1	4	(d)	1	2	4	3

Directions (Q. Nos. 26-29) *Choose the correct demonstrative pronoun.*

26. 

(a) That letter
(b) This letter
(c) These letters
(d) Those letters

27.  

(a) This house
(b) That house
(c) These houses
(d) Those houses

28. 

(a) This apple
(b) Those apples
(c) That apple
(d) These apples

29. 

(a) That bird
(b) Those birds
(c) This bird
(d) These birds

Directions (Q. Nos. 30-32) *Read the passage given below and answer the given questions.*

Leena likes drawing. She attends drawing class once a week with her brother, Shaan. They go to the class riding their bicycles.

Leena's bicycle is red in color. It has a big basket infront. Shaan's bicycle is blue in colour. Both of them make beautiful drawings.

30. How many pronouns are used in the passage?

(a) 4
(b) 6
(c) 7
(d) 8

31. In the passage above 'it' stands for

(a) Shaan's bicycle
(b) Drawing class
(c) Leena's bicycles
(d) Both the bicycles

32. 'Them' used in the last sentence stands for

(a) Both the bicycles
(b) Leena and Shaan
(c) Their drawings
(d) All of the above

Directions (Q. Nos. 33-42) *Given below is a story where some pronouns are missing. Read the story and fill in the blanks with correct pronouns.*

Over a river there was a very narrow bridge. One day a goat was crossing this bridge. Just at the middle of the bridge he met another goat. There was no room for both of ...**(33)**... to pass.

"Go back," said one goat to the other, "there is no room for both of ...**(34)**...".

"Why should I go back ?", said the other goat. "Why should not you go back?"

"...**(35)**... must go back ", said the first goat, "because I am stronger than you."

"You are not stronger than ...**(36)**... ", said the second goat. "...**(37)**... will see about that ", said the first goat, and he put down his horns to fight.

"Stop!", said the second goat. "If we fight, we shall both fall into the river and be drowned. Instead I have a plan. ....**(38)**... shall lie down, and ...**(39)**... may walk over ...**(40)**.... ."

Then the wise goat lay down on the bridge and the other goat walked lightly over ...**(41)**.... . So they passed each other and went on ...**(42)**... ways.

33. (a) him (b) her (c) them (d) their

34. (a) me (b) them (c) us (d) our

35. (a) I (b) He (c) You (d) We

36. (a) me (b) I (c) them (d) you

37. (a) They (b) You (c) We (d) He

38. (a) Me (b) You (c) We (d) I

39. (a) you (b) we (c) they (d) he

40. (a) her (b) me (c) us (d) her

41. (a) him (b) her (c) his (d) their

42. (a) them (b) their (c) his (d) yours

Answers

1. (c)	**2.** (b)	**3.** (a)	**4.** (c)	**5.** (b)	**6.** (a)	**7.** (a)	**8.** (c)	**9.** (b)	**10.** (b)
11. (d)	**12.** (c)	**13.** (d)	**14.** (d)	**15.** (b)	**16.** (c)	**17.** (c)	**18.** (b)	**19.** (b)	**20.** (b)
21. (a)	**22.** (c)	**23.** (b)	**24.** (c)	**25.** (b)	**26.** (b)	**27.** (b)	**28.** (d)	**29.** (b)	**30.** (b)
31. (c)	**32.** (b)	**33.** (c)	**34.** (c)	**35.** (c)	**36.** (a)	**37.** (c)	**38.** (d)	**39.** (a)	**40.** (b)
41. (a)	**42.** (b)								

Verb

Directions (Q. Nos. 1-10) *Choose the verb from the options given below.*

1. (a) Fine (b) Find
   (c) Flower (d) Finger

2. (a) Shame (b) Show
   (c) Snow (d) Scent

3. (a) Coffee (b) Limca
   (c) Drink (d) Orange

4. (a) Laugh (b) Beautiful
   (c) Intelligent (d) Honesty

5. (a) Bubble (b) Burst
   (c) Bonfire (d) Brain

6. (a) Peach (b) Pure
   (c) Paint (d) Pickle

7. (a) Knife (b) Kick
   (c) Crow (d) Cream

8. (a) Scream
   (b) Sour
   (c) Sweet
   (d) Same

9. (a) Big (b) Brown
   (c) Brush (d) Teeth

10. (a) Dish (b) Drive
    (c) Day (d) Car

11. How many verbs are there in the box given below?

    Play, running, teeth, jump, house, drive, cricket, thinking, speak, hate

    (a) 5 (b) 7
    (d) 4 (c) 9

12. *Read the passage given below and answer the given question.*

    My mother wakes up at 5'o clock in the morning. She goes for a walk in the park. She also exercises for some time. Then she comes back and cooks delicious food for us. She packs my tiffin and drops me at the bus stop. I thank my mother for everything.

    How many verbs are used in the passage?

    (a) 6 (b) 10
    (c) 9 (d) 7

Directions (Q. Nos. 13-17) *Identify the verbs from the given sentences.*

13. We flew from New York to Australia.

(a) we (b) from
(c) flew (d) to

14. Mr Das was speaking very loudly.

(a) Mr Das
(b) speaking
(c) very
(d) loudly

15. John and Helen are at school.

(a) and (b) are
(c) at (d) school

16. The tree fell to the ground with a loud noise.

(a) the tree (b) ground
(c) fell (d) loud

17. My family will go to the museum tomorrow.

(a) my family
(b) museum
(c) tomorrow
(d) go

Directions (Q. Nos. 18-22) *Choose the correct helping verb to complete the sentence.*

18. The police .... fight against criminals.

(a) was (b) must
(c) could (d) has

19. My father .... drop us at the venue.

(a) is (b) been
(c) will (d) should

20. My grandparents .... be arriving next month.

(a) will (b) are
(c) were (d) had

21. .... I know who is speaking?

(a) Will (b) Could
(c) Should (d) May

22. Jim and Jack .... performing in the theatre tonight.

(a) are (b) had
(c) have been (d) will

23. Match the following blanks of List I with words in List II.

	List I		List II
A.	My uncle .... to the hospital to meet his mother.	1.	support
B.	The little girl .... her brother to the fair.	2.	believes
C.	Spiderman .... that it is his duty to protect others.	3.	followed
D.	The branches .... our tree house.	4.	rushed

Codes

	A	B	C	D
(a)	2	1	4	3
(b)	3	2	1	4
(c)	4	3	2	1
(d)	2	4	1	3

Directions (Q. Nos. 24-37) *Read the passage given below and complete it by filling in the blanks. Choose the correct answer from the options given below.*

In China there ...**(24)**... a boy who ...**(25)**... to do well in his examinations and ...**(26)**... honour to his parents. One day when he ...**(27)**... for his examination, he ...**(28)**... very sleepy. He ...**(29)**... his head in sleep when his mother ...**(30)**... into the room. His mother ...**(31)**... to wake him up but he did not ...**(32)**... up. This happened every evening when he began to study. His mother ...**(33)**... of a plan. When the boy yawned his mother ...**(34)**... a cord to the end of his pigtail and ...**(35)**... this to a beam in the roof. How did this ...**(36)**... the boy? The pull of the pigtail roused him whenever he ...**(37)**... his eyes to sleep.

24. (a) was lived (b) lived (c) was living (d) has been living

25. (a) wants (b) is wanting (c) wanted (d) has wanted

26. (a) brought (b) is bringing (c) bring (d) was bringing

27. (a) studied (b) was studying (c) studies (d) is studying

28. (a) feel (b) felt (c) was feeling (d) is feeling

29. (a) nodded (b) was nodding (c) nods (d) is nodding

30. (a) enters (b) entering (c) entered (d) was entering

31. (a) tried (b) is trying (c) was trying (d) tries

32. (a) got (b) gets (c) get (d) is getting

33. (a) is thinking (b) thought (c) thinks (d) was thinking

34. (a) tied (b) ties (c) is tieing (d) has tied

35. (a) fastens (b) fastened (c) is fastening (d) has fastened

36. (a) helps (b) helping (c) help (d) had helped

37. (a) closed (b) is closing (c) closes (d) was closing

Answers

1. (b)	2. (b)	3. (c)	4. (a)	5. (b)	6. (c)	7. (b)	8. (a)	9. (c)	10. (b)
11. (b)	12. (c)	13. (c)	14. (b)	15. (b)	16. (c)	17. (d)	18. (b)	19. (c)	20. (a)
21. (d)	22. (a)	23. (c)	24. (b)	25. (c)	26. (c)	27. (b)	28. (b)	29. (b)	30. (c)
31. (a)	32. (c)	33. (b)	34. (a)	35. (b)	36. (c)	37. (a)			

Tense

Directions (Q. Nos. 1-6) *Fill the correct verb to form Simple Present tense in the given sentences.*

1. She usually .... the newspaper in the evening.
(a) read (b) reads
(c) reading (d) readed

2. My mother generally .... delicious food.
(a) cook (b) cooked
(c) cooking (d) cooks

3. They .... a movie every Saturday.
(a) watch (b) watches
(c) watched (d) watching

4. They .... singing everyday.
(a) practised (b) practises
(c) practice (d) practising

5. The Sun .... in the East.
(a) rise (b) rises
(c) rose (d) rised

6. Roshan .... Mathematics in a school.
(a) taught (b) teaching
(c) teaches (d) teached

Directions (Q. Nos. 7-11) *Fill the correct verb to form Simple Past tense in the given sentences.*

7. We .... the problem because the teacher explained it well.
(a) understand (b) understands
(c) understood (d) understanding

8. The cat .... from the table to catch the rat.
(a) jump (b) jumps
(c) jumped (d) jumping

9. The farmer .... money from the moneylender.
(a) borrows (b) borrow
(c) borrowed (d) borrowing

10. James .... the vase in anger.
(a) breaks (b) broken
(c) broke (d) breaked

11. The balloon .... in my hands when I tried to catch it.
(a) bursted (b) bursts
(c) burst (d) bursting

Directions (Q. Nos. 12-16) *Fill the correct verb to form Simple Future tense in the given sentences.*

12. My father .... buy a new house next year.
(a) will (b) is
(c) was (d) are

13. I .... wash the cups. You can dry them.
(a) is (b) shall
(c) was (d) are

14. Susan .... come at 3 o'clock tomorrow.
(a) will (b) was
(c) shall (d) is

15. Look at those black clouds. It .... rain.
(a) was going (b) am going
(c) going (d) will

16. We .... win the match tomorrow if we play well.
(a) shall (b) are
(c) is (d) am

Directions (Q. Nos. 17-21) *Complete the sentences by using the appropriate Simple Present, Past and Future verb forms.*

17. My grandfather .... tea every morning.
(a) cooks (b) drinking
(c) takes (d) having

18. The policeman .... the thief red handed.
(a) catching (b) caught
(c) is catch (d) is caught

19. I think India .... the match tomorrow.
(a) will win
(b) won
(c) is won
(d) had won

20. I .... a client in London yesterday.
(a) is visiting (b) was visiting
(c) visit (d) visited

21. We all .... air, water and food to survive.
(a) needs (b) needed
(c) need (d) will need

22. Match the following in List I with the correct verbs in List II to form Present Continuous tense in the given sentences.

List I	List II
A. We .... a movie right now.	1. am having
B. Dev ..... to his mom on the phone.	2. are watching
C. I ..... severe headache.	3. are making
D. The children ...... a lot of noise.	4. is talking

Codes

	A	B	C	D
(a)	1	3	4	2
(b)	2	4	1	3
(c)	4	2	3	1
(d)	2	4	3	1

Directions (Q. Nos. 23-27) *Fill the correct verb to form Past Continuous tense in the given sentences.*

23. Sita ...... suffering from fever last week.
(a) will (b) was
(c) had (d) were

24. They ...... fighting a lot last night.
(a) are (b) did
(c) were (d) will

25. I ..... to the radio all evening.
(a) am listening
(b) was listening
(c) were listening
(d) listen

26. The light went out while they ..... dinner.

(a) having (b) are having
(c) were having (d) will have

27. The police van ...... the streets whole night.

(a) was patrolling
(b) were patrolling
(c) are patrolling
(d) patrolling

Directions (Q. Nos. 28-32) *Fill the correct verb to form Future Continuous tense in the given sentences.*

28. I .... watching the new movie next week.

(a) was (b) will be
(c) were (d) am

29. My brother .... at home day after tomorrow.

(a) was (b) were
(c) will be (d) is

30. They .... on a pilgrimage soon.

(a) go
(b) were going
(c) are going
(d) shall be going

31. Jack and Ronny .... the tennis match on TV.

(a) will be watching
(b) were watching
(c) are watching
(d) watch

32. Tomorrow evening I .... at the beach in Goa.

(a) will sit (b) will be sitting
(c) was sitting (d) sitting

33. Complete the sentences in List I by using the appropriate Present Continuous, Past Continuous and Future Continuous verb forms in List II.

List I	List II
A. I .... my aunt in the month of December.	1. were speaking
B. The engine ..... a lot of noise.	2. will be visiting
C. They .....very confidently at the seminar last week.	3. are enjoying
D. The children ...... at the party.	4. was making

Codes

	A	B	C	D
(a)	1	3	2	4
(b)	2	1	4	3
(c)	2	4	1	3
(d)	4	3	2	1

Directions (Q. Nos. 34-38) *Identify the correct tense of the following sentences.*

34. He fell asleep while he was driving.

(a) Present continuous
(b) Simple present
(c) Past continuous
(d) Simple future

35. The boy kicks the ball.

(a) Simple present
(b) Simple past
(c) Simple future
(d) None of these

36. Hari is running very fast.

(a) Simple future
(b) Simple past
(c) Present continuous
(d) Simple present

37. He <u>left</u> suddenly without telling or saying any word.

(a) Simple present (b) Simple future
(c) Simple past (d) Present continuous

38. A journalist <u>will come</u> to interview today evening.

(a) Simple present (b) Simple future
(c) Simple past (d) None of these

Directions (Q. Nos. 39-42) *Look at the picture and choose the appropriate sentence with correct tense.*

39.

(a) A painter is painting houses.
(b) A painter paints houses and building.
(c) A painter painted houses and buildings.
(d) A painter will be painting houses and buildings.

40.

(a) A nurse took care of patients.
(b) A nurse is taking care of patients.
(c) A nurse takes care of patients.
(d) A nurse was taking care of patients.

41.

(a) A policeman catches theives and robbers.
(b) A policeman caught theives and robbers.
(c) A policeman was catching theives and robbers.
(d) A policeman will catch theives and robbers.

42.

(a) A dentist is pulling out teeth in his clinic.
(b) A dentist pulls out teeth in his clinic.
(c) A dentist pulled out teeth in his clinic.
(d) A dentist was pulling out teeth in his clinic.

Directions (Q. Nos. 43-50) *Read the passage given below and complete it by filling the blanks.*

Shetty the magician ...**(43)**... home when all of a sudden it began to rain. It ...**(44)**... heavily. Shetty looked around for shelter and ...**(45)**... a pretty little fir tree. He ...**(46)**... towards it as fast as he could. Soon the rain ...**(47)**.... . Shetty was happy that because of the fir tree he did not ...**(48)**... wet. He said to the tree, "Thank you, you have been kind to me. I would like to reward you. ...**(49)**... for any wish and I ...**(50)**... grant it."

43. (a) returned (b) is returning (c) was returning (d) will be returning

44. (a) rained (b) rains (c) raining (d) rain

45. (a) finds (b) find (c) found (d) finded

46. (a) ran (b) running (c) run (d) runs

47. (a) stops (b) stopped (c) stopping (d) is stopping

48. (a) got (b) get (c) gotten (d) gets

49. (a) ask (b) asks (c) asked (d) is asking

50. (a) shall (b) is (c) was (d) am

Answers

1. (b)	2. (d)	3. (a)	4. (c)	5. (b)	6. (c)	7. (c)	8. (c)	9. (c)	10. (c)
11. (c)	12. (a)	13. (b)	14. (a)	15. (d)	16. (a)	17. (c)	18. (b)	19. (a)	20. (d)
21. (c)	22. (b)	23. (b)	24. (c)	25. (b)	26. (c)	27. (a)	28. (b)	29. (c)	30. (d)
31. (a)	32. (b)	33. (c)	34. (c)	35. (a)	36. (c)	37. (c)	38. (b)	39. (a)	40. (c)
41. (a)	42. (a)	43. (c)	44. (a)	45. (c)	46. (a)	47. (b)	48. (b)	49. (a)	50. (a)

Article

Directions (Q. Nos. 1-10) *Fill in the blanks with suitable article.*

1. Iron is .... useful metal.
(a) a
(b) an
(c) the
(d) No article

2. .... Ganga is a sacred river.
(a) A
(b) An
(c) The
(d) No article

3. He is .... honourable man.
(a) a
(b) an
(c) the
(d) No article

4. Please give me........... hammer.
(a) a
(b) an
(c) the
(d) No article

5. .... Sun is very bright today.
(a) A
(b) An
(c) The
(d) No article

6. It takes me .... hour to reach home.
(a) a
(b) an
(c) the
(d) Either 'an' or 'the'

7. Please give me .... ice cream.
(a) a
(b) an
(c) the
(d) No article

8. I liked .... book gifted by you.
(a) a
(b) an
(c) the
(d) Either 'a' or 'the'

9. Please pass me .... plates from the top shelf.
(a) a
(b) an
(c) the
(d) No article

10. English is .... easy.
(a) a
(b) an
(c) the
(d) No article

Directions (Q. Nos. 11-15) *Choose the correct article for the pictures given below.*

11.

Basket

(a) An
(b) A
(c) The
(d) None of these

12.

Octopus

(a) An
(b) A
(c) The
(d) None of these

13.

Old man

(a) An
(b) A
(c) The
(d) None of these

14.

Boxes

(a) A
(b) An
(c) The
(d) None of these

15.

Girl

(a) A
(b) An
(c) The
(d) None of these

Directions (Q. Nos. 16-20) *Choose the sentence with correct use of article.*

16. (a) Please give me orange.
(b) Please give me a orange.
(c) Please give me an orange.
(d) Please give me the orange.

17. (a) It is honour to receive a medal.
(b) It is a honour to receive a medal.
(c) It is an honour to receive a medal.
(d) It is the honour to receive a medal.

18. (a) Europe is smaller than an Asia.
(b) A Europe is smaller than Asia.
(c) An Europe is smaller than Asia.
(d) The Europe is smaller than Asia.

19. (a) Vidisha likes to drink milk.
(b) Vidisha likes to drink a milk.
(c) Vidisha likes to drink an milk.
(d) Vidisha likes to drink the milk.

20. (a) Doctor will come in hour.
(b) Doctor will come in a hour.
(c) Doctor will come in an hour.
(d) Doctor will come in the hour.

Directions (Q. Nos. 21-25) *Fill the blanks with appropriate article.*

21.

.... apple a day keeps the doctor away.

(a) A
(b) An
(c) The
(d) No article

22. 

.... Sun is shining in the East.

(a) A (b) An
(c) The (d) No article

23. 

.... ice cream is more delicious than yogurt.

(a) A (b) An
(c) The (d) No article

24.

Mr John is .... teacher.

(a) a (b) an
(c) the (d) No article

25.

.... egg basket contains five eggs.

(a) A
(b) An
(c) The
(d) No article

26. Match the following sentences in List I with suitable articles in List II.

	List I		List II
A.	.... story that he told me was very interesting.	1.	No article
B.	She is .... student at Barne's School.	2.	an
C.	Jim is ....old friend of mine.	3.	The
D.	My dog does not like .... sweets.	4.	a

Codes

	A	B	C	D
(a)	2	1	3	4
(b)	3	2	4	1
(c)	3	4	2	1
(d)	2	1	4	3

Directions (Q. Nos. 27-31) *Check the usage of articles in the following sentences. Select the correct sequence to the sentences based on Correct (C) /Incorrect (I).*

27. A. Tony got the first prize in the competition.

B. I need an glass of water.

C. I saw a one-eyed man in the circus.

D. He saw the doctor last week.

(a) CCCI (b) CICC
(c) CCII (d) ICIC

28. A. I am going to buy an umbrella.
B. I saw an giraffe in the zoo.
C. He bought a new ball.
D. The tiger is an fast animal.
(a) IICI (b) CCIC
(c) CIIC (d) CICI

29. A. The Taj Mahal is a wonderful monument.
B. My mother will come after an hour.
C. I want the apple.
D. Today is an very important day.
(a) CCII (b) ICCI
(c) CCCI (d) CIII

30. A. I met my cousin the year ago.
B. My grandmother reads the Bhagvad Gita.
C. There is a church on the next street.
D. Children are making the lot of noise.
(a) CCII (b) IICI
(c) ICCI (d) CICC

31. A. It will be an interesting story.
B. The guard opened a door.
C. MS Dhoni is the best cricketer.
D. A Himalayas is the highest mountain range.
(a) CICI (b) ICCI
(c) CCCI (d) IICC

Directions (Q. Nos. 32-39) *Read the passage given below. Fill the blanks to complete the passage from the options given below.*

Last month we went on a trip to ...**(32)**... Middle East. We travelled by ...**(33)**... plane to Cairo. ...**(34)**... Egypt is a fantastic country. We saw pyramids and took boat tour on ...**(35)**... Nile. We had dinner on the boat. It was ...**(36)**... amazing and delicious meal. It was ...**(37)**... best food I have eaten in my life. Overall, ...**(38)**... trip to Egypt was ...**(39)**...wonderful experience.

32. (a) a (b) an
(c) the (d) No article

33. (a) an (b) an
(c) the (d) No article

34. (a) a (b) the
(c) an (d) No article

35. (a) a (b) an
(c) the (d) No article

36. (a) a (b) an
(c) the (d) No article

37. (a) a (b) an
(c) the (d) No article

38. (a) a (b) the
(c) an (d) No article

39. (a) a (b) an
(c) the (d) No article

Answers

1. (a)	**2.** (c)	**3.** (b)	**4.** (a)	**5.** (c)	**6.** (b)	**7.** (b)	**8.** (c)	**9.** (c)	**10.** (d)
11. (b)	**12.** (a)	**13.** (a)	**14.** (d)	**15.** (a)	**16.** (c)	**17.** (c)	**18.** (a)	**19.** (a)	**20.** (c)
21. (b)	**22.** (c)	**23.** (b)	**24.** (a)	**25.** (c)	**26.** (c)	**27.** (b)	**28.** (d)	**29.** (a)	**30.** (c)
31. (a)	**32.** (c)	**33.** (d)	**34.** (d)	**35.** (c)	**36.** (b)	**37.** (c)	**38.** (b)	**39.** (a)	

Adjective

Directions (Q. Nos. 1-5) *Fill in the blanks with an appropriate adjective.*

1. My shoes are really .... so i need new one.
   (a) slow (b) weak
   (c) old (d) hard

2. It is very .... here. Put the lights on.
   (a) bright (b) dark
   (c) calm (d) dull

3. In my country, a few people are rich but many are ....
   (a) unhealthy (b) silent
   (c) poor (d) unhappy

4. He is a good student. He learns very ....
   (a) quietly (b) slow
   (c) studious (d) fast

5. Nike does not like hot tea. He prefers .... milk.
   (a) full (b) cold
   (c) sour (d) tasty

Directions (Q. Nos. 6-11) *Fill in the blanks with suitable adjectives of quantity. Choose from the given options.*

6. His grandfather lost.......... his wealth in the war.
   (a) most (b) no
   (c) all (d) whole

7. Drink .... water before going out in the Sun.
   (a) all (b) some
   (c) most (d) much

8. Is there .... sugar in your tea?
   (a) enough (b) all
   (c) most (d) whole

9. There has not been .... rainfall this year.
   (a) most (b) half
   (c) sufficient (d) many

10. Radha is ill so she did not eat .... rice.
    (a) much (b) any
    (c) all (d) most

11. .... people went to the disco.

(a) No (b) More
(c) Many (d) Much

Directions (Q. Nos. 12-17) *Fill in the blanks with appropriate demonstrative adjectives.*

12. .... boy is very hardworking.

(a) Those (b) That
(c) These (d) Such

13. .... is my handwriting.

(a) These (b) Those
(c) Them (d) This

14. .... sheeps belong to my grandfather.

(a) That (b) Them
(c) Those (d) This

15. My sister baked .... cookies.

(a) that (b) these
(c) them (d) such

16. .... is the Taj Mahal, built by Shahjahan.

(a) That (b) These
(c) Them (d) Such

17. Don't be in .... a hurry.

(a) much
(b) such
(c) many
(d) some

18. Match the following blanks of List I with suitable adjectives of number in List II.

	List I		List II
A.	Humans have .... kidneys.	1.	last
B.	December is the .... month of the year.	2.	many
C.	.... boys like cricket.	3.	two
D.	India has .... cultures.	4.	Most

Codes

	A	B	C	D
(a)	1	3	4	2
(b)	3	1	4	2
(c)	2	4	3	1
(d)	4	2	1	3

Directions (Q. Nos. 19-24) *From the options given, find the adjective corresponding to the word given in capital.*

19. DIRT

(a) Dirtyful (b) Dirtied
(c) Dirty (d) Dirtiable

20. LAUGH

(a) Laughter (b) Laughing
(c) Laughable (d) Laughed

21. PLAY

(a) Playable (b) Playful
(c) Playfully (d) Player

22. FOOL

(a) Foolish (b) Fooling
(c) Fooled (d) Foolable

23. TIRE

(a) Tiring (b) Tirable
(c) Tireless (d) Tired

24. BOY

(a) Boyful (b) Boyable
(c) Boyish (d) Boyhood

Directions (Q. Nos. 25-30) *Which of the following is not an adjective?*

25. (a) Clean (b) Chew
(c) Cheerful (d) Thoughtful

26. (a) Funny (b) Famous
(c) Flew (d) Filthy

27. (a) Broken (b) Busy
(c) Bright (d) Built

28. (a) Green (b) Red
(c) Blue (d) Star

29. (a) Dirty (b) Dinner
(c) Dry (d) Dramatic

30. (a) Lazy (b) Active
(c) Stand (d) Sleepy

Directions (Q. Nos. 31-35) *From the options given below, select the degree of adjective which corresponds to the given word.*

31. Superlative degree

(a) Big (b) Bigger
(c) More big (d) Biggest

32. Positive degree

(a) Hot
(b) Hotter
(c) Hottest
(d) Most hot

33. Comparative degree

(a) Happy (b) Happier
(c) Most happy (d) Happiest

34. Superlative degree

(a) Small (b) More small
(c) Smaller (d) Smallest

35. Positive degree

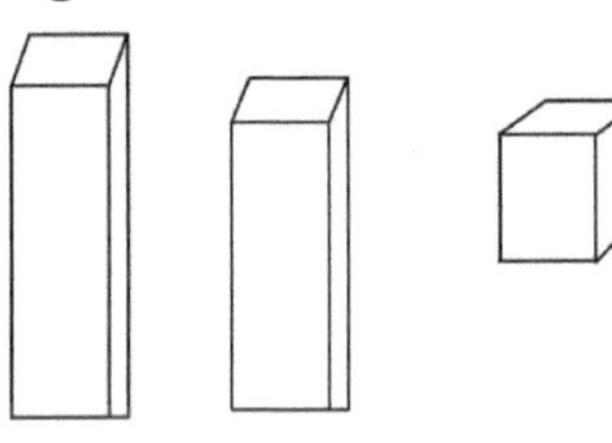

(a) Short (b) Shorter
(c) Most short (d) Shortest

Directions (Q. Nos. 36) *Read the passage given below and answer the given question.*

It was a pleasant day. Rohan visited the beautiful Mughal Gardens. The garden opens once every year for the visitors.

Rohan saw many varieties of flowers in these gardens. Colourful tulips and roses were the main attractions. All the visitors were excited and enjoyed a lot.

36. How many adjectives are used in the passage?
(a) 11 (b) 6
(c) 8 (d) 10

Directions (Q. Nos. 37-45) *Given below is a following cloze passage about Disneyland. Fill the blanks from the options given below.*

Last year I happened to visit Disneyland in Orlando Florida, US. Orlando is one of the ...**(37)**... tourist locations in Florida, perhaps even more than the ...**(38)**... Miami beaches. Many people tend to think that Disneyland is a place for children. This cannot be ...**(39)**... from the truth. Disneyland is one of the ...**(40)**... and ...**(41)**... amusement parks in the world. The Disneyland Orlando is also known as the Magic kingdom and this is a ...**(42)**... name for the place. It is of no surprise that many adults have found Disneyland to be extremely ...**(43)**.... Even though ...**(44)**... of the rides are meant for the children, they can be ...**(45)**... for adults also as really marvellous. Magic kingdom is an architectural piece of wonderland.

37. (a) busier (b) most busy (c) busy (d) busiest

38. (a) famous (b) infamous (c) well known (d) popular

39. (a) farther (b) farthest (c) further (d) most farther

40. (a) large (b) largest (c) larger (d) most large

41. (a) prominent (b) more prominent (c) prominence (d) most prominent

42. (a) perfect (b) more perfect (c) most perfect (d) perfection

43. (a) entertain (b) entertained (c) entertainment (d) entertaining

44. (a) much (b) many (c) most (d) more

45. (a) pleasure (b) pleasurable (c) pleased (d) pleasing

Answers

1. (c)	2. (b)	3. (c)	4. (d)	5. (b)	6. (c)	7. (b)	8. (a)	9. (c)	10. (b)
11. (c)	12. (b)	13. (d)	14. (c)	15. (b)	16. (a)	17. (b)	18. (b)	19. (c)	20. (c)
21. (b)	22. (a)	23. (d)	24. (c)	25. (b)	26. (c)	27. (d)	28. (d)	29. (b)	30. (c)
31. (d)	32. (a)	33. (b)	34. (d)	35. (a)	36. (c)	37. (d)	38. (a)	39. (c)	40. (b)
41. (d)	42. (a)	43. (d)	44. (c)	45. (d)					

Adverb

Directions (Q. Nos. 1-6) *Fill in the blanks with appropriate adverbs.*

1. 

The baby is sleeping ....

(a) brightly (b) peacefully
(c) neatly (d) slowly

2. 

The man is dressed ....

(a) loudly (b) early
(c) neatly (d) easily

3. 

The Sun is shining ....

(a) peacefully (b) frequently
(c) already (d) brightly

4. 

The milkman delivers milk ....

(a) daily (b) sadly
(c) loudly (d) neatly

5. 

The man is driving ....

(a) unhappily
(b) suddenly
(c) joyfully
(d) carefully

6. 

The musician plays ....

(a) partly (b) easily
(c) melodiously (d) angrily

Directions (Q. Nos. 7-11) *Fill in the blanks with appropriate adverbs of manner from the options given below.*

7. The jackal howls ....

(a) quickly (b) slowly
(c) loudly (d) brightly

8. We ate food ....

(a) sadly (b) hungrily
(c) beautifully (d) softly

9. Tina saw a lizard and ran out ....

(a) loudly
(b) quickly
(c) neately
(d) angrily

10. Kitty waited for the food ....

(a) patiently (b) easily
(c) completely (d) correctly

11. The scientist performed the experiment ....

(a) merrily
(b) noisily
(c) softly
(d) carefully

Directions (Q. Nos. 12-16) *Complete the sentences by chosing appropriate adverbs of place from the options given below.*

12. Please park your car........ .

(a) everywhere (b) outside
(c) behind (d) forward

13. The jar is kept .... the cupboard.

(a) above
(b) here
(c) away
(d) everywhere

14. The taxi dropped us .... from the venue.

(a) forward (b) inside
(c) under (d) far away

15. Tall students were asked to stand........ .

(a) below (b) forward
(c) behind (d) everywhere

16. We could not find Sohan ....

(a) everywhere (b) anywhere
(c) somewhere (d) here

Directions (Q. Nos. 17-21) *Identify the adverb of time in the given sentences.*

17. My family will go to the museum today.

(a) my family
(b) will go
(c) museum
(d) today

18. Taj Mahal was built many years ago.

(a) Taj Mahal (b) built
(c) many (d) year

19. He comes home very late.

(a) he (b) late
(c) comes (d) very

20. He called here a few minutes ago.

(a) He called (b) here
(c) few (d) ago

21. The judges arrived before the chief guest.

(a) arrived
(b) before
(c) chief guest
(d) None of the above

Directions (Q. Nos. 22-26) *Fill in the blanks with appropriate adverbs of degree from the options given below.*

22. I .... go out with my friends.

(a) fully (b) almost
(c) often (d) ever

23. I am confident as I am .... prepared for the exam.

(a) rarely (b) fully
(c) quite (d) partly

24. The senior surgeon remains .... busy.

(a) quite (b) ever
(c) enough (d) rather

25. We had .... time to relax.

(a) often (b) enough
(c) any (d) almost

26. These mangoes are .... ripe.

(a) often
(b) rarely
(c) no
(d) ever

27. Match the sentences in List I with appropriate adverbs of frequency in List II.

List I		List II	
A.	We celebrate Diwali ..... in a year.	1.	twice
B.	We should ..... try to help others.	2.	once
C.	My aunt visits us	3.	always
D.	We should brush ..... in a day.	4.	frequently

Codes

	A	B	C	D
(a)	1	3	4	2
(b)	2	4	3	1
(c)	2	3	4	1
(d)	3	2	1	4

Directions (Q. Nos. 28-30) *Find out the interrogative adverbs from the given options.*

28. (a) Don't (b) Where
(c) Now (d) Within

29. (a) Whole (b) Much
(c) When (d) High

30. (a) Why (b) Fully
(c) Once (d) Again

Directions (Q. Nos. 31-39) *Read the passage given below which has some blanks. Fill in blanks to complete the passage from the options given below.*

Last night, Sohan had a ...**(31)**... sleep. In the morning, he woke up ...**(32)**... his alarm rang. He felt fresh and energetic. He dressed up ...**(33)**.... He could see the Sun shining ...**(34)**... from his window. His mother had prepared the breakfast ...**(35)**... and called him to come downstairs ...**(36)**... .

Sohan was ...**(37)**... late for school. He was sure that he would catch the school bus. He grabbed his bag and moved ...**(38)**... to the bus stop. He reached the school and went ...**(39)**... his classroom.

31. (a) quickly (b) everyday (c) sound (d) slowly

32. (a) loudly (b) before (c) partly (d) very

33. (a) neatly (b) soon (c) certainly (d) never

34. (a) twice (b) often (c) half (d) brightly

35. (a) clearly (b) already (c) beautifully (d) daily

36. (a) noisily (b) quickly (c) sadly (d) quite

37. (a) rarely (b) now (c) merrily (d) after

38. (a) everywhere (b) often (c) swiftly (d) inside

39. (a) partly (b) always (c) again (d) inside

Directions (Q. No. 40) *Read the passage given below and answer the question given below.*

Abhishek went to the hospital yesterday. His aunt is unwell. He visits here frequently. In the hospital we should speak softly and politely. We should not disturb other patients.

40. How many adverbs are used in the above passage?
(a) 3 (b) 4
(c) 6 (d) 7

Answers

1. (b)	2. (c)	3. (d)	4. (a)	5. (d)	6. (c)	7. (c)	8. (b)	9. (b)	10. (a)
11. (d)	12. (b)	13. (a)	14. (d)	15. (c)	16. (b)	17. (d)	18. (c)	19. (b)	20. (c)
21. (b)	22. (c)	23. (b)	24. (a)	25. (b)	26. (b)	27. (c)	28. (b)	29. (c)	30. (a)
31. (c)	32. (b)	33. (a)	34. (d)	35. (b)	36. (b)	37. (a)	38. (c)	39. (d)	40. (b)

Conjunction

Directions (Q. Nos. 1-10) *Fill in the blanks with an appropriate conjunction.*

1. John is a Canadian .... his wife is an Indian.
(a) and (b) or
(c) but (d) yet

2. It was raining .... I took an umbrella.
(a) and (b) because
(c) or (d) so

3. I could cook some dinner .... we could order some pizza.
(a) and (b) or
(c) but (d) so

4. This service is free .... they charge money.
(a) and (b) but
(c) yet (d) so

5. You can go to the tourist office .... ask for the information.
(a) and (b) because
(c) yet (d) but

6. We can enter the theatre .... we reach on time.
(a) yet (b) but
(c) if (d) because

7. He phoned me .... he needed someone to talk to.
(a) for (b) but
(c) and (d) so

8. I could not spend time with my family .... I was very busy.
(a) and (b) but
(c) because (d) so

9. You can .... come with me to the library .... stay at home.
(a) neither, nor (b) either, or
(c) but, and (d) and, or

10. I like fresh fruits .... not green vegetables.
(a) and (b) but
(c) yet (d) for

Directions (Q. Nos. 11-14) *Choose the conjunction in the given sentences.*

11. The novel in English was long but very interesting.
(a) novel (b) long
(c) but (d) interesting

12. Paul and Claire like to swim.

(a) like (b) to
(c) and (d) Both 'a' and 'c'

13. He is sick yet he wants to go out.

(a) he (b) sick
(c) yet (d) go out

14. The school bus driver wanted to turn right but had to turn left instead.

(a) bus driver (b) but
(c) turn (d) wanted

15. Find out the number of conjunctions in the box given below. Choose the correct answer from the option given below.

building	and	but	if
Sonam	or	Dr Sharma	table
so	through	because	church

(a) 5 (b) 6
(c) 7 (d) 9

16. Match the following blanks of List I with words in List II.

List I	List II
A. They are not having dinner ..... they had a heavy lunch.	1. or
B. Lara cannot take part in the race ..... she has a partner.	2. but
C. Do you want to read a book ..... watch television?	3. unless
D. Sunil was looking for his pen ..... could not find it.	4. because

	A	B	C	D		A	B	C	D
(a)	2	1	4	3	(b)	4	2	1	3
(c)	3	1	4	2	(d)	4	3	1	2

Directions (Q. Nos. 17-21) *Choose the correct statement from the options given below.*

17. (a) I like to run and not walk.
(b) I like to run yet not walk.
(c) I like to run but not walk.
(d) I like to run so not walk.

18. (a) Is that tiger and leopard?
(b) Is that tiger but leopard?
(c) Is that tiger or leopard?
(d) Is that tiger for leopard?

19. (a) Either Ram nor Rani will go to the circus.
(b) Either Ram and Rani will go to the circus.
(c) Either Ram or Rani will go to the circus.
(d) Either Ram but Rani will go to the circus.

20. (a) We bought a cake so my brother's birthday.
(b) We bought a cake for my brother's birthday.
(c) We bought a cake since my brother's birthday.
(d) We bought a cake because my brother's birthday.

21. (a) Jatin scored full marks because he worked hard.
(b) Jatin scored full marks but he worked hard.
(c) Jatin scored full marks or he worked hard.
(d) Jatin scored full marks and he worked hard.

Directions (Q. Nos. 22-27) *Given below is a dialogue between Mike and Peter with some blanks. Complete the dialogue by choosing the correct conjunction.*

Mike Let's go out in the evening.
Peter I'm sorry, I can't meet you today ...**(22)**... I'm busy. I can meet you tomorrow ...**(23)**... Saturday.
Mike Tomorrow I am busy ...**(24)**... I can't come. Is Saturday OK?
Peter Sure, I am free all day so let's go out!
Mike Do you like flying?
Peter No, I don't.
Mike Why not?
Peter ...**(25)**... I can't sleep well ...**(26)**... airports are really boring.
Mike Right. The first time airports are really exciting ...**(27)**... , then they lose their charm and become boring.
Peter OK, then we are meeting on Saturday.
Mike Oh sure!

22. (a) as (b) because
(c) for (d) All of these

22. (a) as (b) because (c) for (d) All of these

23. (a) and (b) or (c) nor (d) yet

24. (a) yet (b) but (c) so (d) and

25. (a) Because (b) But (c) So (d) Or

26. (a) or (b) and (c) so (d) because

27. (a) and (b) but (c) or (d) so

Directions (Q. Nos. 28-35) *Given below is a passage with some blanks, where conjunctions are missing. Fill the blanks from options given below.*

Once we were locked out ...**(28)**... we had lost our keys. Mom was at Grandma's house. She would come home early ...**(29)**... we could phone her and let her know ...**(30)**... we could not use our phone as the house was locked. ...**(31)**... we decided to go to Mrs Jone's house who lived next door. We rang her bell and she called out to wait as she was busy. We were waiting for her ...**(32)**... dad came home early. He was very unhappy ...**(33)**... gave the other set of keys to open the house.

We were really thrilled ...**(34)**... relaxed. A warning of course! Came from father ...**(35)**... we start taking care of our own things we would be in trouble as we were today.

28. (a) but (b) since (c) because (d) Both 'b' and 'c'

29. (a) though (b) if (c) but (d) because

30. (a) and (b) or (c) but (d) if

31. (a) And (b) So (c) But (d) Or

32. (a) till (b) until (c) since (d) but

33. (a) and (b) but (c) since (d) or

34. (a) so (b) but (c) and (d) if

35. (a) although (b) if (c) but (d) unless

Answers

1. (c)	2. (d)	3. (b)	4. (c)	5. (a)	6. (c)	7. (a)	8. (c)	9. (b)	10. (b)
11. (c)	12. (c)	13. (c)	14. (b)	15. (c)	16. (d)	17. (c)	18. (c)	19. (c)	20. (b)
21. (a)	22. (a)	23. (b)	24. (c)	25. (a)	26. (b)	27. (b)	28. (d)	29. (b)	30. (c)
31. (b)	32. (b)	33. (b)	34. (c)	35. (d)					

Preposition

Directions (Q. Nos. 1-5) *Fill the blanks with appropriate prepositions of place from the option given below .*

1.

Fruits are .... the basket.

(a) on (b) in
(c) under (d) over

2.

The books are .... the table and the chair.

(a) inside
(b) among
(c) between
(d) under

3.

The books are .... the table.

(a) on (b) over
(c) under (d) in

4.

The ball is .... the box.

(a) under
(b) behind
(c) near
(d) over

5. 

The dog is .... the table.

(a) over (b) on
(c) in (d) under

Directions (Q. Nos. 6-10) *Choose the correct sentence according to the given picture.*

6. 

(a) The pig is under a sty.
(b) A pig is on a sty.
(c) A pig is in a sty.
(d) A pig is over a sty.

7. 

(a) A pup is on a cot.
(b) A pup is in a cot.
(c) A pup is under a cot.
(d) A pup is over the cot.

8. 

(a) A glass is beside the table.
(b) A glass is in the table.
(c) A glass is on the table.
(d) A glass is under the table.

9. 

(a) The cat is sleeping behind the chair.
(b) The cat is sleeping next to the chair.
(c) The cat is sleeping under the chair.
(d) The cat is sleeping beside the chair.

10. 

(a) Bees are flying at the flowers.
(b) Bess are flying in the flowers.
(c) Bees are flying over the flowers.
(d) Bees are flying around the flowers.

Directions (Q. Nos. 11-15) *Fill in the blanks with appropriate prepositions of time from the options given below.*

11. I have been waiting for the courier .... last week.

(a) for (b) after
(c) since (d) at

12. My mother told us to be home .... 10 o'clock.

(a) during
(b) by
(c) between
(d) under

13. I will visit my hometown .... my vacations.

(a) during (b) before
(c) upon (d) along

14. Children must have meals .... time.

(a) after (b) on
(c) past (d) during

15. The patients waited .... the doctor arrived.

(a) from (b) onto
(c) since (d) until

Directions (Q. Nos. 16-20) *Fill in the blanks with appropriate prepositions of movement from the options given below.*

16. I am going .... the post office.

(a) from (b) to
(c) at (d) up

17. The car brushed .... the footpath.

(a) against (b) between
(c) after (d) into

18. Suddenly, a puppy came .... the street.

(a) until (b) off
(c) out of (d) upon

19. Can you please move the screen .... your right.

(a) up (b) towards
(c) through (d) along

20. The teacher asked the children to sit ....

(a) from (b) upon
(c) past (d) down

Directions (Q. Nos. 21-25) *Find out the option which is not a preposition.*

21. (a) With (b) Among
(c) Yet (d) Above

22. (a) In (b) At
(c) On (d) Because

23. (a) Above (b) Over
(c) Among (d) And

24. (a) To (b) Of
(c) In (d) But

25. (a) Under (b) Inside
(c) So (d) Behind

Directions (Q. Nos. 26-29) *Fill in the blanks with suitable prepositions from the options given below.*

26. When will you arrive .... the office.

(a) in (b) to
(c) at (d) on

27. Kids are playing .... the garden.

(a) outside (b) in
(c) above (d) over

28. I think she spent the whole afternoon .... the phone.

(a) in (b) at
(c) on (d) over

29. You can come .... with us .

(a) into (b) upon
(c) along (d) past

30. Find out the number of prepositions in the box given below. Choose the correct answer from the given options.

on	but	if	after	between	infront
at	before	and	since	inside	box
ball	clouds	near	driving	house	father
temple	along	into	behind	under	above

(a) 10 (b) 14
(c) 18 (d) 20

31. Match the picture with proper preposition and complete the sentence.

List I		List II
A.	A coat is ..... he hanger.	1. inside/in
B.	 The snail is jumping ....the box.	2. down
C.	 The dog is ..... the box.	3. over
D. 	 The man fell ..... the stairs.	4. on

Codes

	A	B	C	D
(a)	2	1	3	4
(b)	4	3	1	2
(c)	2	1	4	2
(d)	1	2	3	4

Directions (Q. Nos. 32-36) *Given below is a picture. Look at the picture and answer the questions by choosing the correct option.*

32. The man is sitting .... an office chair.

(a) in (b) at
(c) on (d) over

33. The pile of books is .... the table.

(a) on (b) around
(c) next to (d) near

34. The books are .... the book case.

(a) on (b) in
(c) at (d) of

35. The cheese cake is kept .... the book case.

(a) at
(b) above
(c) on
(d) in

36. The mouse is going ....of the open door.

(a) in
(b) out
(c) towards
(d) through

Directions (Q. Nos. 37-45) *Read the passage given below. Fill the blanks to complete the passage from the options given below.*

My family is going ...**(37)**... Agra. We will stay there ...**(38)**... my school reopens. We are on a train. We started our journey ...**(39)**... Delhi. There are few stations ...**(40)**... Delhi and Agra. I am sitting ...**(41)**... the window. My parents are sitting ...**(42)**... me. My sister is sitting ...**(43)**... them. I am looking ...**(44)**... the window. There are many farms and fields. The train will soon pass ...**(45)**... a tunnel. I am enjoying the train journey.

37. (a) in (b) to (c) at (d) since

38. (a) around (b) over (c) until (d) to

39. (a) from (b) along (c) on (d) upon

40. (a) towards (b) between (c) near (d) through

41. (a) near (b) over (c) inside (d) from

42. (a) behind (b) above (c) against (d) in

43. (a) below (b) between (c) after (d) past

44. (a) out of (b) inside (c) upon (d) against

45. (a) over (b) through (c) around (d) with

Answers

1. (b)	**2.** (c)	**3.** (a)	**4.** (c)	**5.** (d)	**6.** (c)	**7.** (a)	**8.** (c)	**9.** (c)	**10.** (c)
11. (c)	**12.** (b)	**13.** (a)	**14.** (b)	**15.** (d)	**16.** (b)	**17.** (a)	**18.** (c)	**19.** (b)	**20.** (d)
21. (c)	**22.** (d)	**23.** (d)	**24.** (d)	**25.** (c)	**26.** (c)	**27.** (b)	**28.** (c)	**29.** (c)	**30.** (b)
31. (b)	**32.** (c)	**33.** (d)	**34.** (b)	**35.** (c)	**36.** (b)	**37.** (b)	**38.** (c)	**39.** (a)	**40.** (b)
41. (a)	**42.** (a)	**43.** (b)	**44.** (a)	**45.** (b)					

Punctuation

Directions (Q. Nos. 1-10) *Fill the blanks with the correct punctuation mark to make meaningful sentences.*

1. Do you know where is Ram ....
(a) . (b) ?
(c) ! (d) ,

2. Wow .... look at the fireworks.
(a) ! (b) ?
(c) . (d) ;

3. Sara ate pizza for lunch ....
(a) - (b) ?
(c) . (d) !

4. I purchased an apple .... banana and a mango.
(a) , (b) !
(c) : (d) ?

5. Long live the king ....
(a) , (b) !
(c) . (d) :

6. Kartik is my best friend ....
(a) ? (b) ;
(c) : (d) .

7. I can speak English .... Hindi and French.
(a) ? (b) !
(c) , (d) .

8. Bravo .... You are a genious.
(a) ! (b) ?
(c) . (d) ;

9. Reading .... listening to music and travelling are some of my hobbies.
(a) ! (b) ,
(c) : (d) ?

10. Who is hiding behind the door ....
(a) . (b) ,
(c) ! (d) ?

Directions (Q. Nos. 11-16) *Find the correct sentence in the following options.*

11. (a) How long will you be gone!
(b) How long will you be gone?
(c) How long will you be gone.
(d) How long will you be gone;

12. (a) Miss Benny? May I use your telephone?
(b) Miss Benny! May I use your telephone!
(c) Miss Benny, May I use your telephone?
(d) Miss Benny, May I use your telephone.

13. (a) Bill added, they are eating all the peanuts.
(b) Bill added they are eating all the peanuts?
(c) Bill added. they are eating all the peanuts.
(d) Bill added, "they are eating all the peanuts".

14. (a) The fruit seller sells apples oranges mangoes etc.
(b) The fruits seller sells apples, oranges, mangoes, etc.
(c) The fruit seller sells apples; oranges; mangoes etc.
(d) The fruit seller, sells apples mangoes etc.

15. (a) Alas! What a terrible fire!
(b) Alas. What a terrible fire.
(c) Alas, what a terrible fire!
(d) Alas; what a terrible fire

16. (a) Hardwork honesty and self-confidence lead to success.
(b) Hardwork, honesty and self-confidence lead to success.
(c) Hardwork, honesty, self-confidence, lead to success.
(d) Hardwork, honesty, self-confidence lead to success?

Directions (Q. Nos. 17-21) *Select the sentence which is written incorrectly.*

17. (a) Nick will reach Delhi on Friday.
(b) He will visit the Red fort Qutab Minar Raj Ghat Chandhi Chowk.
(c) Red Fort, Qutab Minar and Chandni Chowk are located in Central Delhi.
(d) Nick asked, "How far is Qutab Minar from Central Delhi?"

18. (a) Summer, winter, autumn and spring are the four main seasons.
(b) Each season has its unique charm.
(c) In the spring season flowers blossom fresh leaves grow its lush green everywhere.
(d) Leaves become orange and yellow during autumn.

19. (a) Alas The great poet is no more.
(b) He suffered from cancer.
(c) The loss is great!
(d) His poems, stories and letters are widely read.

20. (a) Sam woke up in the morning.
(b) He said, "What a lovely day!"
(c) O! He had to go to school.
(d) He had not finished his maths science english homework

21. (a) My mother is cooking dinner.
(b) She needs butter, rice, flour, etc.
(c) She asked me, "Where is the jam?"
(d) I said I do not know.

22. Match the sentences in List I with appropriate punctuation marks in List II.

List I	List II
A. Could you please give me that book	1. (!)
B. This is extraordinary	2. (.)
C. My aunt will come tomorrow	3. (?)
D. I ordered a pizza a burger and some chips.	4. (,)

Codes

	A	B	C	D
(a)	3	1	2	4
(b)	1	3	4	2
(c)	3	2	1	4
(d)	2	3	4	1

Directions (Q. Nos. 23-30) *Given below is a paragraph which is without use of punctuation marks. Read the paragraph and use comma, exclamation mark, question mark and full stop where required.*

I have a dog ...**(23)**... He is a labrador. He is black in colour ...**(24)**... has big ears and a long tail. He wags his tail and licks my face when he is happy ...**(25)**... He loves going for walks. I take him to school sometimes. He is friends with a bulldog ...**(26)**.... a german shepherd and a pug ...**(27)**... Once he saw a black cat and wanted to chase her too.

O Lord ...**(28)**... He is as swift as an eagle. He also likes to look at the children playing in the garden ...**(29)**... I wish I could spend all my time with him ...**(30)**...

23. (a) question mark (b) full stop (c) comma (d) exclamation mark

24. (a) full stop (b) comma (c) exclamation mark (d) semi colon

25. (a) exclamation mark (b) comma (c) question mark (d) full stop

26. (a) full stop (b) exclamation mark (c) question mark (d) comma

27. (a) comma (b) exclamation mark (c) full stop (d) question mark

28. (a) exclamation mark (b) question mark (c) full stop (d) comma

29. (a) comma (b) exclamation mark (c) full stop (d) question mark

30. (a) full stop (b) question mark (c) comma (d) semi colon

Answers

1. (b)	2. (a)	3. (c)	4. (a)	5. (b)	6. (d)	7. (c)	8. (a)	9. (b)	10. (d)
11. (b)	12. (c)	13. (d)	14. (b)	15. (a)	16. (b)	17. (b)	18. (c)	19. (a)	20. (d)
21. (d)	22. (a)	23. (b)	24. (b)	25. (d)	26. (d)	27. (c)	28. (a)	29. (c)	30. (a)

Jumbled Words and Sentences

Directions (Q. Nos. 1-10) *Given below are jumbled words. Unscramble the names of these interesting sports. Choose the correct answer from the options given below.*

1. TKSIANG
(a) Skeeing (b) Skating
(c) Skipping (d) Skiing

2. LWOBIGN
(a) Gobling (b) Bating
(c) Bowling (d) Gliding

3. BOFTOALL
(a) Volleyball (b) Football
(c) Baseball (d) Ball

4. IDNIGV
(a) Driving (b) Winning
(c) Giving (d) Diving

5. RIKCETC
(a) Ticker (b) Ticket
(c) Cricket (d) Wicket

6. CHEYOK
(a) Tennis (b) Kayaking
(c) Cockyeh (d) Hockey

7. JDUO
(a) Doju (b) Dodge
(c) Judo (d) Judge

8. OXNBIG
(a) Bignox (b) Bowling
(c) Balling (d) Boxing

9. GIHNKI
(a) Biking (b) Hiking
(c) Viking (d) Niking

10. SCSEH
(a) Chess (b) Cheese
(c) Seech (d) Cash

Directions (Q. Nos. 11-18) *Given below are words in jumbled manner. Frame an appropriate word from the words. Choose the correct answer from the options given below.*

11. PTERMOCU
(a) Compacter (b) Computer
(c) Pomcuret (d) Morpetcu

12. NGOEDL
(a) Noegde
(b) Longed
(c) Dongle
(d) Both 'b' and 'c'

13. CKTIHNE
(a) Tiknitch (b) Chicken
(c) Kitchen (d) Kitten

14. RASIMLI
(a) Rasmili (b) Similar
(c) Misalir (d) Misilar

15. UGBRER
(a) Rubber (b) Burger
(c) Rubger (d) Grubber

16. REPTYT
(a) Terry (b) Party
(c) Pretty (d) Plenty

17. RHEBOTR
(a) Bottle (b) Bowler
(c) Bother (d) Brother

18. LEPCNI
(a) Lentil (b) Pencil
(c) Penny (d) Picnic

Directions (Q. Nos. 19-23) *Given below are jumbled words. Frame proper words by selecting the combination of numbers.*

19. R O R S Y
1 2 3 4 5
(a) 2 4 1 3 5 (b) 4 2 1 3 5
(c) 5 4 1 2 3 (d) 2 3 4 1 5

20. A C R H I
1 2 3 4 5
(a) 4 5 1 2 3 (b) 2 3 4 5 1
(c) 1 4 5 2 3 (d) 2 4 1 5 3

21. P A E R P
1 2 3 4 5
(a) 4 5 1 2 3 (b) 1 2 5 3 4
(c) 3 1 2 4 5 (d) 5 4 1 2 3

22. O N I U S C
1 2 3 4 5 6
(a) 4 5 6 1 3 2 (b) 3 2 1 6 5 4
(c) 6 1 4 5 3 2 (d) 5 6 3 2 1 4

23. T C A H E
1 2 3 4 5
(a) 2 3 4 5 1 (b) 1 5 3 2 4
(c) 3 1 5 4 2 (d) 2 4 5 1 3

24. Match the jumbled words and their photos in List I with their correct spellings in List II.

List I	List II
A. SURNE	1. Birthday
B. RMPHGAONE	2. Nurse
C. RHAIBTDY	3. Ostrich
D.  GDRAIEN	4. Gramophone
E.  SRHOTIC	5. Reading

Codes

	A	B	C	D	E
(a)	4	2	1	3	5
(b)	2	4	1	5	3
(c)	1	4	3	2	5
(d)	3	2	1	4	5

Directions (Q. Nos. 25-34) *Rearrange the words to form meaningful sentences.*

25. boy / is / an / the / eating / apple
(a) Eating an the apple is boy.
(b) The boy is eating an apple.
(c) The boy eating an apple is.
(d) An apple is eating the boy.

26. play / everyday / cricket / we
(a) Play cricket we everyday.
(b) Everyday cricket we play.
(c) We play cricket everyday.
(d) Play everyday we cricket.

27. is / medicine / laughter / best / the
(a) Laughter is the best medicine.
(b) Medicine is the best laughter.
(c) Best laughter is the medicine.
(d) The best medicine is laughter.

28. shines / the / day / during / Sun / the
(a) The day shines during Sun the.
(b) Shines the day during the Sun.
(c) The Sun during shines the day.
(d) The Sun shines during the day.

29. honesty / best / the / policy / is
(a) Policy best the honesty is.
(b) Honesty is the best policy.
(c) Best is the policy honesty.
(d) The policy honesty is best.

30. the / wear / please / belt / seat
(a) Seat belt wear the please.
(b) Belt wear the seat please.
(c) Please wear the seat belt.
(d) Please seat wear the belt.

31. brother / not / my / feeling / is / well
(a) Not feeling my brother is well.
(b) Is feeling my brother not well.
(c) Brother my not is feeling well.
(d) My brother is not feeling well.

32. like / play / computer / to / I / games
(a) I like to play computer games.
(b) I play computer like to games.
(c) Play computer games I like to.
(d) Computer play games I like to.

33. Robert Frost / a / famous / is / poet
(a) Famous poet is Robert Frost a.
(b) Robert Frost is a famous poet.
(c) Poet is a Robert Frost famous.
(d) Is poet a Robert Frost famous.

34. mobile / switch / your / off / phone
(a) Your switch off mobile phone.
(b) Mobile phone off switch your.
(c) Switch off your mobile phone.
(d) Switch your mobile off phone.

35. Arrange the sentences in the proper logical order to form a meaningful story.
Me and milk
1. Milk is an important source of calcium.
2. Today I had science period in the school.
3. It also keeps teeth healthy and the skin glowing.
4. My teacher taught us the advantages of having milk everyday.
5. I will go home and drink milk.
6. It makes the bones strong and healthy.
7. I finished the whole glass.
8. She added chocolate powder in the milk.
9. I will become healthy and strong now.
10. I asked my mother to give me a glass of milk.

Codes
(a) 1, 2, 4, 3, 6, 7, 5, 9, 8, 10
(b) 2, 4, 1, 6, 3, 5, 10, 8, 7, 9
(c) 3, 5, 6, 9, 7, 8, 2, 1, 4, 10
(d) 10, 1, 4, 2, 6, 3, 5, 8, 9, 7

Answers

1. (b)	**2.** (c)	**3.** (b)	**4.** (d)	**5.** (c)	**6.** (d)	**7.** (c)	**8.** (d)	**9.** (b)	**10.** (a)
11. (b)	**12.** (d)	**13.** (c)	**14.** (b)	**15.** (b)	**16.** (c)	**17.** (d)	**18.** (b)	**19.** (b)	**20.** (d)
21. (b)	**22.** (c)	**23.** (b)	**24.** (b)	**25.** (b)	**26.** (c)	**27.** (a)	**28.** (d)	**29.** (b)	**30.** (c)
31. (d)	**32.** (a)	**33.** (b)	**34.** (c)	**35.** (b)					

Word Power

Directions (Q. Nos. 1-10) Find *the synonym of the given word. Choose the correct answer from the given options.*

1. Alien
(a) Native (b) Common
(c) Tenant (d) Foreigner

2. Hop
(a) Walk (b) Jump
(c) Lie down (d) Stand

3. Packed
(a) Lonely (b) Heavy
(c) Crowded (d) Light

4. Terrible
(a) Sweet (b) Incredible
(c) Horror (d) Horrible

5. Charming
(a) Right (b) Attractive
(c) Sorrow (d) Incorrect

6. Active
(a) Vast
(b) Dull
(c) Energetic
(d) None of the above

7. Enormous
(a) Tiny (b) Large
(c) High (d) Similar

8. Eager
(a) Wise (b) Sober
(c) Unwise (d) Curious

9. Cold
(a) Freezing (b) Harsh
(c) Hot (d) Liquid

10. Foe
(a) Friend (b) Relative
(c) Enemy (d) Brother

Directions (Q. Nos. 11-15) *Choose the synonym of the underlined word.*

11. He gifted me a very <u>expensive</u> watch.
(a) cheap
(b) costly
(c) huge
(d) shiny

12. Jack is an <u>industrious</u> boy.
(a) smart (b) energetic
(c) hard-working (d) happy

13. I don't <u>remember</u> where I met Kate.
(a) shallow (b) forget
(c) analyse (d) recall

14. The show was very <u>entertaining</u>.
(a) dull (b) funny
(c) enjoyable (d) boring

15. The sum was <u>difficult</u>.
(a) tight (b) narrow
(c) tough (d) wide

Directions (Q. Nos. 16-25) *Find the antonym of the given word. Choose the correct answer from the given options.*

16. Mean
(a) Happy (b) Tall
(c) Weird (d) Nice

17. Misplace
(a) Ignore (b) Find
(c) Question (d) Loud

18. Overlook
(a) Notice (b) Lose
(c) Upset (d) Ignore

19. Noisy
(a) Find (b) Little
(c) Loud (d) Quiet

20. Excited
(a) Calm (b) Lose
(c) Upset (d) Quiet

21. Tight
(a) Thin (b) Right
(c) Loose (d) Apart

22. Sad
(a) Excited (b) Comical
(c) Dumb (d) Gloomy

23. Visible
(a) Near (b) Invisible
(c) Clear (d) Vision

24. Broad
(a) Wide (b) Fade
(c) Distant (d) Narrow

25. Alive
(a) Lively (b) Energy
(c) Dead (d) Awake

Directions (Q. Nos. 26-30) *Choose the antonym for the underlined words.*

26. The soldier was very clever and <u>brave</u>.
(a) bright (b) fat
(c) smart (d) coward

27. The teacher asked us to stay away from <u>dangerous</u> places.
(a) hazardous (b) risky
(c) safe (d) plenty

28. My father is the <u>eldest</u> son of his family.
(a) oldest
(b) stubborn
(c) youngest
(d) polite

29. Richa did not <u>accept</u> my invitation.
(a) rude (b) agree
(c) receive (d) deny

30. It started raining as soon as I <u>entered</u> the school.
(a) come (b) exit
(c) celebrate (d) join

Directions (Q. Nos. 31-40) *Choose the word on the right that best expresses a relationship similar to that of the original pair.*

31. Fire : Hot : : Snow : ?
(a) Frozen (b) Yellow
(c) Warm (d) Tasty

32. Spend : Save : : Give : ?
(a) Watch (b) Receive
(c) Say (d) Ask

33. Brush : Paint : : Pen : ?
(a) Eat (b) Steal
(c) Write (d) Have

34. Race : Competition : : Party : ?
(a) Career (b) Preparation
(c) Game (d) Celebration

35. Mother : Female : : Father : ?
(a) Angry (b) Kind
(c) Male (d) Thin

36. Wall : Room : : ?
(a) Lettuce : Sandwich (b) Dog : Cat
(c) Wheel : Car (d) Song : Dance

37. Candy : Sweet : : ?
(a) Water-Frozen (b) Time : Fast
(c) Money-Rich (d) Fire : Hot

38. Finger : Hand : : ?
(a) Tomato : Sandwich (b) Dog : Eat
(c) Leaf : Tree (d) Shoe : Socks

39. Day : Month : : ?
(a) Year : Minute
(b) Second : Minute
(c) Time : Pass
(d) Study : Book

40. Smell : Nose : : ?
(a) Ear : Tongue
(b) Body : Human
(c) Sight : Eye
(d) Finger : Arm

Directions (Q. Nos. 41-55) *Find the odd one out from the options given below.*

41. (a) Milk (b) Tea
(c) Coffee (d) Banana

42. (a) Gold (b) Silver
(c) Copper (d) Water

43. (a) Fish (b) Frog
(c) Dog (d) Crocodile

44. (a) Bed (b) Bucket
(c) Bottle (d) Cup

45. (a) Run (b) Jump
(c) Pasta (d) Walk

46. (a) Pen (b) Paper
(c) Pencil (d) Chair

47. (a) Fruits (b) Milk
(c) Chicken (d) Vegetables

48. (a) Bulb (b) Light
(c) Lamp (d) Clock

49. (a) Milk (b) Rice
(c) Yoghurt (d) Cheese

50. (a) Monday (b) January
(c) March (d) May

51. (a) Foot ball (b) Hockey
(c) Cooking (d) Cricket

52. (a) Red (b) Yellow
(c) Pink (d) Heavy

53. (a) Apple (b) Orange
(c) Onion (d) Banana

54. (a) Walking (b) Sleeping
(c) Running (d) Jogging

55. (a) Rose (b) Potato
(c) Lily (d) Sunflower

Directions (Q. Nos. 56-60) *Find the odd one out from the figures given below.*

Directions (Q. Nos. 61-85) *Select the one word which substitutes the given sentence.*

61. A person who looks after sick patients.
(a) Lawyer (b) Teacher
(c) Doctor (d) Writer

62. A person who does not eat chicken or fish.
(a) Non-vegetarian (b) Vegetarian
(c) Vegetable (d) Inedible

63. A person who lives next door.
(a) Neighbour (b) Family
(c) Students (d) Relatives

64. A person who mends shoes.
(a) Jeweller (b) Helper
(c) Plumber (d) Cobbler

65. A person who flies aeroplanes.
(a) Pilot (b) Astronaut
(c) Engineer (d) Astronomer

66. A person who cures your toothache.
(a) Physiotherapist
(b) Counsellor
(c) Dentist
(d) Mechanic

67. A person who manages work.
(a) Nurse (b) Manager
(c) Mason (d) Guard

68. A person who repairs pipes and leakages.
(a) Plumber (b) Carpenter
(c) Magician (d) Chemist

69. A person who acts in movies and serials.
(a) Musician (b) Director
(c) Singer (d) Actor

70. A person who makes furniture.
(a) Carpenter (b) Artist
(c) Designer (d) Leader

71. A person who writes books.
(a) Driver (b) Author
(c) Printer (d) Doctor

72. A person who writes poems.
(a) Singer (b) Dancer
(c) Poet (d) Musician

73. A person who sells medicines.
(a) Plumber (b) Guard
(c) Teacher (d) Chemist

74. A person who cannot read and write.
(a) Electrician (b) Illiterate
(c) Literate (d) Milkman

75. A person who makes clothes.

(a) Tailor (b) Carpenter
(c) Cobbler (d) Writer

76. A place where criminals are kept.

(a) School (b) Zoo
(c) Prison (d) Society

77. A person who paints walls and houses.

(a) Helper (b) Painter
(c) Driver (d) Electrician

78. A person who takes care of plants and flowers.

(a) Gardener
(b) Tailor
(c) Architect
(d) Lawyer

79. A person who delivers milk everyday.

(a) Cobbler
(b) Singer
(c) Milkman
(d) Florist

80. A person who manages books in the library.

(a) Teacher (b) Librarian
(c) Dancer (d) Receptionist

81. A person who cooks food in a restaurant.

(a) Chef (b) Waiter
(c) Painter (d) Singer

82. A person who cuts hair.

(a) Cabbler (b) Plumber
(c) Tailor (d) Barber

83. A place where you go to worship.

(a) School (b) Market
(c) Temple (d) Office

84. A place where you go to exercise.

(a) Parlour (b) Gym
(c) Mall (d) Tution

85. A place where you go out to eat.

(a) Restaurant (b) Church
(c) Garden (d) Hospital

Answers

1. (d)	**2.** (b)	**3.** (c)	**4.** (d)	**5.** (b)	**6.** (c)	**7.** (b)	**8.** (d)	**9.** (a)	**10.** (c)
11. (b)	**12.** (c)	**13.** (d)	**14.** (c)	**15.** (c)	**16.** (d)	**17.** (b)	**18.** (a)	**19.** (d)	**20.** (a)
21. (c)	**22.** (d)	**23.** (b)	**24.** (d)	**25.** (c)	**26.** (d)	**27.** (c)	**28.** (c)	**29.** (d)	**30.** (b)
31. (a)	**32.** (b)	**33.** (c)	**34.** (d)	**35.** (c)	**36.** (c)	**37.** (d)	**38.** (c)	**39.** (b)	**40.** (c)
41. (d)	**42.** (d)	**43.** (c)	**44.** (a)	**45.** (c)	**46.** (d)	**47.** (c)	**48.** (d)	**49.** (b)	**50.** (a)
51. (c)	**52.** (d)	**53.** (c)	**54.** (b)	**55.** (b)	**56.** (c)	**57.** (a)	**58.** (d)	**59.** (d)	**60.** (d)
61. (c)	**62.** (b)	**63.** (a)	**64.** (d)	**65.** (a)	**66.** (c)	**67.** (b)	**68.** (a)	**69.** (d)	**70.** (a)
71. (b)	**72.** (c)	**73.** (d)	**74.** (b)	**75.** (a)	**76.** (c)	**77.** (b)	**78.** (a)	**79.** (c)	**80.** (b)
81. (a)	**82.** (d)	**83.** (c)	**84.** (b)	**85.** (a)					

Reading Comprehension

Passage 1

Directions (Q. Nos. 1-5) *Given below is a paragraph. Read it and answer the questions that follow from the options given below.*

Jeddi and his Kangaroo

Long ago, in a desert outside the city, lived Jeddi, a young boy.

Jeddi and his father were out hunting one day when they saw a baby Kangaroo lying on the ground.

Jeddi said, "It's hurt Dad."

"Yes it is," said Jeddi's father, "Shall we help it?"

"Yes," said Jeddi.

Jeddi and his father took the Kangaroo back to their camp in the desert.

Each day they gave the Kangaroo some food to eat and some water to drink. After about three weeks the Kangaroo was well again.

Jeddi said to the Kangaroo, "Now you are better...you are free to hop away and go back to the other Kangaroos."

Do you think the Kangaroo hopped away? No, it stayed with Jeddi and became his pet.

1. Jeddi lived with his father in a ....

(a) big city
(b) far away in the desert
(c) in a huge house
(d) near the sea-shore

2. What did Jeddi and his father find out while hunting one day?

(a) A bag full of money
(b) A trapped lion
(c) A small Kangaroo lying hurt
(d) A small bird bleeding

3. Why do you think the Kangaroo stayed with Jeddi?
   (a) Kangaroo liked deserts
   (b) Other animals became his friends
   (c) Jeddi and Kangaroo became good friends
   (d) Kangaroo was no more

4. An antonym of the word 'young' can be
   (a) new (b) away
   (c) old (d) better

5. A synonym of the word 'hurt' can be
   (a) hopped (b) hoped
   (c) injured (d) heated

Passage 2

Directions (Q. Nos. 1-5) *Read the poem and answer the questions that follow. Choose the correct answer from the options given below.*

Lovely Things

Bread is a lovely thing to eat -
God bless the barley and the wheat!
A lovely thing to breathe is air -
God bless the sunshine everywhere!
The Earth's a lovely place to know -
God bless the folks that come and go!
Alive's a lovely thing to be -
Giver of life - we say - bless Thee!

HM Sarson

1. What makes bread a lovely thing to eat?
   (a) Rice (b) Barley
   (c) Wheat (d) Both 'b' and 'c'

2. What makes air a lovely thing to breathe?
   (a) Bread (b) God
   (c) Sunshine (d) All of these

3. In the poem, what is the other name used to refer to God?
   (a) Folks (b) Giver of life
   (c) Bless Thee (d) Alive

4. The meaning of the word 'folks' will be
   (a) people (b) non-living things
   (c) birds (d) plants and trees

5. The antonym of the word 'alive' will be
   (a) shivering (b) burried
   (c) thinking (d) dead

Passage 3

Directions (Q. Nos. 1-5) *Read the passage and answer the questions that follow. Choose the correct answer from the options given below.*

Once upon a time there was a hungry fox. One night he was searching for some food. He met a little kitten and was tempted to eat her. When he tried to pounce on the kitten, the kitten said, 'Oh, don't eat me. I know where the farmer keeps his cheese. Come with me and see.'

The kitten lead him into the farmyard, where there was a deep well. 'Now, look in here and you will see the cheese,' she said.

The fox looked down the well and saw the moon reflected in the water. He thought it was a cheese ball. The foolish fox jumped into the well and was drowned.

1. How did the fox feel when he saw the kitten?
   (a) He thought of making the kitten his friend
   (b) He was tempted to eat the kitten
   (c) He thought of playing with the kitten
   (d) He wanted to kill the kitten

2. Where did the kitten take the fox?
   (a) To the forest (b) To her home
   (c) To the farmyard (d) To the Lion king

3. What did the fox find in the well?
   (a) A cheese cake
   (b) Reflection of the moon
   (c) Hot water
   (d) A bucket

4. The meaning of the word 'pounce' will be to
   (a) sit there (b) jump and catch
   (c) suddenly (d) run away

5. The antonym of the word 'foolish' will be
   (a) comic (b) serious
   (c) wise (d) strong

Passage 4

Directions (Q. Nos. 1-5) *Read the poem and answer the questions that follow. Choose the correct answer from the options given below.*

Little white lily
Sat by a stone,
Drooping and waiting
Till the sun shone.
Little white lily
Sunshine has fed;
Little white lily
Is lifting her head.
Little white lily
Droops with pain,
Waiting and waiting
For the wet rain.
Little white lily
Holds her cup;
Rain is fast falling
And filling it up.

—George MacDonald

1. Where is little white lily sitting?
   (a) By a wall (b) By a stone
   (c) In the flower pot (d) By a window

2. When did little white lily lift her head?
   (a) When it received sunshine
   (b) When it received air
   (c) When it woke up
   (d) When it was happy

3. Why does little white lily hold her cup?
   (a) To receive sunshine (b) To receive oxygen
   (c) To pass it on (d) To receive rainwater

4. The antonym of the word 'wet' will be
   (a) liquid (b) dry
   (c) moist (d) watery

5. The synonym of the word 'shine' will be
   (a) smooth (b) dull
   (c) sparkle (d) creamy

Passage 5

Directions (Q. Nos. 1-5) *Read the poem and answer the questions that follow. Choose the correct answer from the options given below.*

My Teacher Took My iPod

My teacher took my iPod.
She said they had a rule;
I couldn't bring it into class
or even to the school.
She said she would return it;
I'd have it back that day.
But then she tried my headphones on
and gave a click on Play.
She looked a little startled,
but after just a while
she made sure we were occupied
and cracked a wicked smile.
Her body started swaying .
Her toes began to tap.
She started grooving in her seat
and rocking to the rap.
My teacher said she changed her mind.
She thinks it's now okay
to bring my iPod into class.
She takes it every day.

—Kenn Nesbitt

1. What action of the poet was against the school rules?
   (a) To talk to other students
   (b) Sing in the class
   (c) To bring iPod to the class
   (d) To sleep in the class

2. Why did the teacher change her mind about the iPod?
   (a) She thought rule was wrong
   (b) She liked clicking the play-button
   (c) She liked listening to it
   (d) She was hungry

3. How often does the teacher take the student's iPod?
   (a) Every week (b) Never
   (c) Every day (d) Every other day

4. In the line 'she looked a little startled'. The word 'startled' will mean
   (a) happy (b) surprised
   (c) angry (d) sad

5. Antonym of the word 'grooving' will be
   (a) jumping up and down
   (b) sitting seriously
   (c) miserable
   (d) upbeat

Passage 6

Directions (Q. Nos. 1-5) *Read the passage and answer the questions that follow. Choose the correct answer from the options given below.*

Once a teacher and a drummer were resting under a tree in the forest. It was a hot day and they were exhausted. Suddenly, they heard a movement in the bushes. They turned and jumped to their feet. A tiger stood there before them. The drummer was extremely scared but the teacher remained calm. The drummer was shocked and asked, 'Why aren't you scared? My hands and legs are shivering.'

The teacher replied, 'Don't show that you are scared or else the tiger will eat you up. Don't move or else the tiger will pounce upon you. Be calm and all will be well.'

1. What made the tired teacher and drummer turn around?
   (a) A gun shot
   (b) A lion roar
   (c) A movement in the bushes
   (d) A wolf howl

2. How was the drummer's reaction different from that of the teacher?
   (a) Both of them were scared
   (b) The teacher was scared but the drummer remained calm
   (c) The drummer was scared but the teacher remained calm
   (d) The drummer ran away

3. What did the teacher advice to the drummer?
   (a) Hurry and run away
   (b) Fight the tiger
   (c) Be calm and all will be well
   (d) Start crying

4. The synonym of the word 'exhausted' will be
   (a) hot (b) tired
   (c) active (d) bored

5. The meaning of the word 'shivering' will be
   (a) cold (b) hot
   (c) stiff (d) shaking

Answers

Passage 1	1. (b)	2. (c)	3. (c)	4. (c)	5. (c)
Passage 2	1. (d)	2. (c)	3. (b)	4. (a)	5. (d)
Passage 3	1. (b)	2. (c)	3. (b)	4. (b)	5. (c)
Passage 4	1. (b)	2. (a)	3. (d)	4. (b)	5. (c)
Passage 5	1. (c)	2. (c)	3. (c)	4. (b)	5. (b)
Passage 6	1. (c)	2. (c)	3. (c)	4. (b)	5. (d)

Practice Set 1

1. Match the subjects in List I with their predicates in List II.

List I		List II	
A.	Rajan	1.	went to catch the thief.
B.	They	2.	is a small house.
C.	Ours	3.	is preparing for his exam.
D.	Their	4.	country is the best.

Codes

	A	B	C	D
(a)	3	1	4	2
(b)	4	3	2	1
(c)	3	4	1	2
(d)	3	1	2	4

2. Choose the correct abstract noun for the word 'Wise'.
(a) Wisdom (b) Wiseness
(c) Wise (d) Wiseful

3. Choose the correct interogative pronoun to complete the given sentence.
.... do you want to meet?
(a) Who (b) What
(c) Whom (d) Whose

4. Choose the correct helping verb to complete the sentence.
Tendulkar .... play cricket when he was 3.
(a) would (b) could
(c) should (d) shall

5. Fill in the blank with a suitable adjective.
Aalok is the .... boy in his class.
(a) tall (b) taller
(c) more tall (d) tallest

6. Complete the blank by using the correct form of the verb in the bracket.
I .... (study) when Rohan came to meet me.
(a) was studying (b) were studying
(c) studied (d) am studying

7. Check the usage of articles in the following sentences. Select the correct sequence to the sentences based on Correct (c)/Incorrect (I).
A. Rashi had a banana for breakfast.
B. A Elephant is a huge animal.
C. An honest man is liked by all.
D. An India is a big country.
(a) CICC (b) CCCC
(c) CICI (d) ICIC

8. Fill in the blank with appropriate adverb.
Rohan .... waited for the exam result.
(a) quickly (b) brickly
(c) eagerly (d) blindly

9. Fill in the blank with appropriate conjunction.
We will go to the beach .... play there.
(a) and (b) but
(c) or (d) nor

10. Find the odd-one out from the following.
(a) Inside (b) Above
(c) With (d) Yet

11. Which of the following sentence is properly punctuated?
(a) Diwali is a festival of Hindus.
(b) Kajal, Karita and Naina went to a party.
(c) MS Dhoni is the captain of Indian cricket team.
(d) I like to play, read books, watch movies and go for shopping in my free time.

12. Unscramble the following to make a meaningful word.
YGRBU
(a) RUBGY (b) RUGBY
(c) RUYGB (d) RUGYB

13. Rearrange the following words to make a meaningful sentence.
city/our/It/duty/keep/is/to/clean/our
(a) It is duty our keep to our city clean.
(b) It is our duty to keep our city clean.
(c) It is our city to keep our duty clean.
(d) It is our duty to keep city clean our.

14. Choose the antonym of the underlined word in the sentence.
We waited for the flight to <u>depart</u>.
(a) arrived (b) arrive
(c) reach (d) go

15. The synonym of the word 'hike' is
(a) down
(b) decrease
(c) reduce
(d) increase

16. Find the odd-one out.
(a) Land (b) Sun
(c) Moon (d) Clouds

17. Choose the word on the right that best expresses a relationship similar to that of the words on the left.
Ice : Cream :: Fire : ?
(a) Flue (b) Flew
(c) Fly (d) Far

18. Punctuate the following sentence properly.
Rahims Bag is full of books toys and mobiles,
(a) Rahim's bag is full of books, toys and mobliles.
(b) Rahims bag is full of books, toys and mobiles.
(c) Rahim's bag is full of books toys and mobile's.
(d) rahim's bag is full of books, toys and mobiles.

19. Find the verbs in the following sentence.
The cat caught the mouse and ran away.
(a) caught
(b) ran
(c) cat
(d) caught, ran

20. Find the collective noun in the following sentence.
A small family is a happy family.
(a) small (b) family
(c) happy (d) None of these

Directions (Q. Nos. 20-25) *Read the passage and answer the questions given below.*

Rano was Anika's pet cat. She played with Rano after coming home from school. One day Anika got late in coming from school. She had participated in the sports day and had to stay back at school for practice. Rano kept waiting at the entrance for Anika to arrive. She did not have food and was worried about Anika. Anika's mother tried to tell her that Anika would be late but animals can't understand our language. She started playing with Rano but Rano didn't budge from the gate. Finally, Anika arrived and Rano ran to sit on her lap. They both were very happy to see each other.

21. When did Anika play with Rano?
(a) Before going to school.
(b) During the school hours.
(c) After coming back from school.
(d) While Anika's mother was sleeping.

22. Anika participated in
(a) the Annual Day. (b) a poetry competition.
(c) a dance competition. (d) the Sports Day.

23. Where did Rano wait?
(a) At the entrance of Anika's house.
(b) In Anika's bedroom.
(c) In Anika's studyroom.
(d) In the courtyard.

24. The opposite of 'entrance' is
(a) excite (b) exit
(c) end (d) out

25. The words 'didn't budge' mean
(a) didn't eat (b) didn't play
(c) didn't sleep (d) didn't move

Answers

1. (d)	**2.** (a)	**3.** (c)	**4.** (b)	**5.** (d)	**6.** (a)	**7.** (c)	**8.** (c)	**9.** (a)	**10.** (d)
11. (d)	**12.** (b)	**13.** (b)	**14.** (c)	**15.** (d)	**16.** (a)	**17.** (c)	**18.** (a)	**19.** (d)	**20.** (b)
21. (c)	**22.** (d)	**23.** (a)	**24.** (b)	**25.** (d)					

Practice Set 2

1. Fill in the blank with a suitable collective noun.
My mother asked me to carry the .... of newspapers to the store room.
(a) bunch (b) herd
(c) bundle (d) bouquet

2. What is the abstract noun of 'Modest'?
(a) Modern (b) Mode
(c) Model (d) Modesty

3. Match the following.

List I		List II	
A.	It	1.	clothes are missing.
B.	She	2.	are coming now.
C.	They	3.	is going to school.
D.	Their	4.	rained yesterday.

Codes

	A	B	C	D		A	B	C	D
(a)	1	2	3	4	(b)	4	2	3	1
(c)	4	3	2	1	(d)	3	4	1	2

4. Fill in the blank with a suitable adjective.
The student fell down. His school bag was very ....
(a) light (b) small
(c) heavy (d) strong

5. Fill in the blank using appropriate adjective.
Nadia can run as .... as Komal.
(a) fastly (b) faster
(c) fastest (d) fast

6. Use the correct form of the verb in the bracket to fill in the blank.
The thief was .... (catch) by the police in no time.
(a) catch (b) caught
(c) catching (d) catched

7. Fill in the blank with a suitable helping verb.
All drivers .... obey traffic rules.
(a) could (b) will
(c) must (d) has

8. Which of the following sentence is in Simple Future tense?
(a) The Sun sets in the East.
(b) She went to her class.
(c) I will have finished my homework by this time tomorrow.
(d) My father will go to Mumbai tomorrow.

9. Identify the sentence in which articles are used properly.
(a) A monkey went to an hotel.
(b) A apples are good for everyone.
(c) An almirah was shifted from this room.
(d) A honest man is praised by all.

10. Fill in the blank with a suitable article.
Sunita left .... hour ago.
(a) a (b) an
(c) the (d) No article

11. Fill in the blank with a suitable adverb.
My friend can speak French ....
(a) loudly (b) quickly
(c) neatly (d) fluently

12. Fill in the blank with a suitable conjunction.
The man is poor, ... he is honest.
(a) and (b) but
(c) if (d) because

13. Choose the correct sentence.
(a) We can buy a t-shirt if we buy a coat for Rahul.
(b) We can either buy a t-shirt or a coat for Rahul.
(c) We can buy a t-shirt because we buy a coat for Rahul.
(d) We can buy a t-shirt yet we buy a coat for Rahul.

14. Which of the following is not a preposition?
(a) Behind (b) On
(c) But (d) Above

15. Which sentence is punctuated properly?
(a) Navin, Pravin and Shirin are playing Golf,
(b) Navin, Pravin and Shirin are playing golf.
(c) Navin, Pravin and shirin are playing Golf.
(d) Navin Pravin and Shirin are playing golf.

16. Frame a meaningful word from the given letters.
NIBLDUIG
(a) Budding (b) Building
(c) Digging (d) Double

17. Rearrange the words to form a meaningful sentence.
to/but/we/late/the/were/train/catch/got/able
(a) We late got were but able to catch the train.
(b) We got late but able were to catch the train.
(c) We got late but were able to catch the train.
(d) We were able to catch the train got late but.

18. Find the odd-one out.
(a) Cold drink (b) Cold coffee
(c) Soup (d) Lemonade

19. The antonym of the underlined word in the sentence is
We should prevent cruelty against animals.
(a) kind (b) kindly
(c) reality (d) kindness

20. The synonym of 'greedy' is
(a) unselfish (b) selfish
(c) moral (d) immoral

Directions(Q. Nos. 21-25) *Read the passage and answer the questions from the options given below.*

The Bee

Bees live in a house that is called a hive. There are three kinds of bees: Workers, drones and queens. Only one queen bee can live in each hive. If she is lost or dead, the other bees will stop their work.

Bees are very wise and busy little creatures. They all join together to build cells of wax for their honey. Each bee takes its proper place and does its own work. Some go out and gather honey from the flowers; others stay at home and work inside the hive.

The cells which they build are all of one shape and size, and no room is left between them. The cells are not round. They have six sides.

Did you ever look into a glass hive to see the bees while at work? It is pleasant to see how busy they always are. But the drones do not work. Before winter comes, all the drones are driven from the hive so that they don't eat the honey which they did not gather.

It is not safe for children to handle bees. Bees have a painful sting that they use in their defense.

21. How many queen bees can live in a hive?
(a) Two queen bees (b) Only one queen bee
(c) Four queen bees (d) No queen bee

22. What is not true about the wax cells built by the bees?
(a) The cells are of the same shape and size.
(b) The cells have a lot of space between them.
(c) The cells are not round.
(d) The cells have six sides.

23. Why are drones driven out of the hives?
(a) Drones are busy little creatures.
(b) Drones find winters unpleasant.
(c) Drones sting others.
(d) Drones did not work to gather honey.

24. An antonym of the word 'dead' will be
(a) alive (b) deadly
(c) buried (d) energetic

25. A synonym of the word 'gather' will be
(a) consume (b) save
(c) collect (d) distribute

Answers

1. (c)	**2.** (d)	**3.** (c)	**4.** (c)	**5.** (d)	**6.** (b)	**7.** (c)	**8.** (d)	**9.** (c)	**10.** (b)
11. (d)	**12.** (b)	**13.** (b)	**14.** (c)	**15.** (b)	**16.** (b)	**17.** (c)	**18.** (c)	**19.** (d)	**20.** (b)
21. (b)	**22.** (b)	**23.** (d)	**24.** (a)	**25.** (c)					

Practice Set 3

1. Match the following subjects with their predicates.

	Subject		Predicate
A.	A Doctor	1.	went to a party.
B.	I	2.	pet is missing.
C.	My	3.	invented the bulb.
D.	Edison	4.	treats patients.

Codes

	A	B	C	D
(a)	4	1	3	2
(b)	2	1	4	3
(c)	4	1	2	3
(d)	1	2	3	4

2. Identify the common noun in the sentence.
A bird came inside my room.
(a) came (b) inside
(c) room (d) bird

3. Fill in the blank with suitable pronouns.
God helps ...... who help ....
(a) these, them (b) those, themselves
(c) those, themself (d) that, themselves

4. Find the verb(s) in the following sentence.
The birds kept on singing, cuddling and kissing.
(a) singing (b) cuddling
(c) kissing (d) All of these

5. Fill in the correct verb to form Past Continuous Tense in the sentence.
I ...... a cricket match last night.
(a) watched (b) was watching
(c) were watching (d) watching

6. Choose the sentence with the correct use of articles.
(a) An ant and a grasshopper became friends.
(b) A ant and an grasshopper became friends.
(c) A ant came to meet an grasshopper.
(d) An ant came to meet an grasshopper.

7. Fill in the blank with suitable adjective of quantity.
You can take ...... cookies from the plate.
(a) any (b) much
(c) most (d) some

8. Identify the adverb in the sentence.
The quick, brown fox jumped lazily on the dog.
(a) lazily (b) quick
(c) brown (d) on

9. Complete the sentence using appropriate conjunction.
Make hay .... the Sun shines.
(a) and (b) while
(c) but (d) or

10. Identify the preposition(s) in the sentence.
I kept the book on the table but somebody kept it under it.
(a) on (b) under
(c) on, under (d) but

11. Find the correctly punctuated sentence from the following.
(a) Kamal went to a Party Today.
(b) Shahid and Mira got married last year.
(c) Wow! What a great catch!
(d) I like to eat chocolates,

12. Rearrange the following letters to make a meaningful word.
OLBIEM
(a) MOLIBE (b) MELOBI
(c) MEOLIB (d) MOBILE

13. Rearrange the following words to make a meaningful sentence.
dog's/Nandu/is/pet/name/my
(a) My dog's pet is name Nandu.
(b) My dog's name pet is Nandu.
(c) My name pet dog's is Nandu.
(d) My pet dog's name is Nandu.

14. What is the antonym of the underlined word in the sentence?
He went to a noisy park.
(a) quiet (b) quite
(c) quick (d) naughty

15. Choose the word on the right that best expresses a relation similar to that on the left pair.
Ball : Play : : Pen : ....
(a) White (b) Write
(c) Study (d) Read

16. Fill in the blank using the appropriate collective noun.
A .... of bees was hovering over the flowers.
(a) herd (b) flock
(c) swarm (d) army

17. The abstract noun of 'brave' is
(a) braveness (b) bravity
(c) brevity (d) bravery

18. Fill in the blank using the correct form of adjective.
Honey is .... than sugar.
(a) sweet (b) sweetest
(c) sweeter (d) more sweet

19. Choose a suitable preposition to fill the blank.
The train went .... the tunnel.
(a) in
(b) across
(c) between
(d) through

20. Fill in the blank using articles.
.... Octopus is .... acquatic animal.
(a) An, an (b) A, an
(c) A, a (d) The, the

Directions (Q. Nos. 21-25) *Read the passage and answer the questions given below.*

Teepu had a bad day. He was punished by his class teacher as he had not completed his homework. The teacher asked him to go out of the class. She also wrote a note in his diary which he had to get signed from his parents. When Teepu reached home form school, he was scared to show the note to his parents. He did not know what to do. If he did not get it signed, he would not be allowed to attend the class tomorrow. He planned to sign the note himself.

21. Why was Teepu punished?
(a) Because he completed his homework.
(b) Because he came late to class.
(c) Because he did not complete his homework.
(d) Because he did not complete his classwork.

22. What did Teepu's teacher do?
(a) She wrote a note in Teepu's diary.
(b) She punished Teepu.
(c) She took the class to a picnic.
(d) Both 'a' and 'b'

23. Who had to sign the note in Teepu's diary?
(a) Teepu's father (b) Teepu's parents
(c) Teepu's brother (d) Teepu's grandparents

24. The antonym of 'punished' is
(a) praised (b) scolded
(c) scored (d) befriended

25. He planned to sign the note himself.
In the above sentence, 'he' stands for
(a) Teepu's father (b) Teepu's class teacher
(c) Teepu's brother (d) Teepu

Answers

1. (c)	2. (d)	3. (b)	4. (d)	5. (b)	6. (a)	7. (d)	8. (a)	9. (b)	10. (c)
11. (c)	12. (d)	13. (d)	14. (a)	15. (b)	16. (c)	17. (d)	18. (c)	19. (d)	20. (a)
21. (c)	22. (d)	23. (b)	24. (a)	25. (d)					

9 789350 944295

Printed by Libri Plureos GmbH in Hamburg,
Germany